Lavalette Perrin

The records of the General association of the colony of Connecticut

Lavalette Perrin

The records of the General association of the colony of Connecticut

ISBN/EAN: 9783337101701

Printed in Europe, USA, Canada, Australia, Japan

Cover: Foto ©ninafisch / pixelio.de

More available books at **www.hansebooks.com**

THE RECORDS

OF THE

GENERAL ASSOCIATION

OF Y^e

COLONY OF CONNECTICUT.

Begun June 20th, 1738.
Ending June 19th, 1799.

———•♦•———

HARTFORD, CONN.:
PRESS OF THE CASE, LOCKWOOD & BRAINARD COMPANY.
1888.

PREFACE.

The General Association of Connecticut, at its meeting in Rockville, June 21, 1887, appointed Messrs. E. B. Hillard, J. H. Twichell, and F. S. Hatch a committee to ask the General Conference to publish the manuscript Minutes of the General Association, a copy of which is deposited in Memorial Hall.

At the suggestion of this committee, the General Conference, on the 9th of November following, passed this resolution at its meeting in Middletown:

"*Resolved*, That it is desirable that the unpublished records of the General Association of Connecticut be published; and it is hereby ordered that they be published under the superintendence of a committee to be appointed by the General Conference, in such way as it shall provide; and that a copy of the minutes so published be furnished to every Congregational minister, and every Congregational church in the State."

Messrs. Lavalette Perrin, William DeL. Love, Jr., and Charles H. Clark, were appointed a committee to execute this resolution.

This committee in consultation agreed upon a literal transcript of the records, retaining as much as possible the peculiarities of the times as indicated by the record book itself, and assigned the labor of preparing for the press, and executing the details of publication, to their chairman.

The result is given in the volume now presented to the churches, and only a few words of explanation are called for in this connection.

Any one who has made the attempt will understand the difficulty of transcribing ancient documents, so as to retain the peculiarities of spelling, punctuation, and capitals, with other unique items which give the flavor of antiquity to the text, and pay no deference to modern grammatical rules.

As far as possible the editor has endeavored to retain the appearance of the old record book in this volume.

PREFACE.

The Notes, the Index of names, and the Index of topics, are the result of no little care and labor on the part of the editor, and of course are no part of the original Records as found in the Book, but are added to render the volume more available for reference.

While there will be found some errors and defects in the book, it is hoped they are not so numerous or serious as to hinder its usefulness, or provoke needless criticism.

The reader who has the candor to place himself in the circumstances of the actors, will look in vain through these records for marks of such bigotry as some have attributed to our fathers. On the contrary, the circumstances being duly considered, a sincerity and nobility of character mark the doings here recorded, for which all candid readers will be thankful to God, who gave us such an ancestry.

The churches of the State are indebted to a few liberal individuals and churches, for the means with which to place these records within the reach of all who desire to consult them. The money thus freely given may be regarded as a tribute to the memory of the fathers, and a boon to coming generations.

LAVALETTE PERRIN.

Torrington, Aug. 13, 1888.

1738.

At a convention of the General Association of the Colony of Connecticut, at Stratford in the County of Fairfield on the 20th day of June 1738

Present

The Rev.d
1. Mr. William Burnham, Modr.
2. Mr. Jacob Hemingway
3. Mr. Samuel Cook
4. Mr. Hezekiah Gold
5. Mr. Thomas Clap, Scribe
6. Mr. Thomas Ruggles
7. Mr. Ashbel Woodbridge
8. Mr. Elnathan Whitman
9. Mr. Ephraim Bostwick
10. Mr. William Hart.

Voted & Resolved, that there shall be a Convention of the General Association of this Colony, consisting of Two Delegates from each Perticular Association, to meet in the several Counties successively in the following Order, viz: in the Counties of Fairfield, New Haven, Hartford, Windham & New London, & at such Towns in the said Counties as the Association shall from time to time appoint; on the Third Tuesday in June, annually at eleven of the clock in the forenoon: Whose Work & Business according to our Ancient Constitution & Practice, is & shall be, To take care of & Inspect the General State of Religion, to Promote Unity & Order in our Ecclesiastical Affairs, & to Recommend to the Consideration of the Particular Associations such matters & things as they shall Apprehend to be for the General Good. And that the Particular Association in whose Bounds the General

Association shall be convened, shall appoint a Minister to Preach a Public Lecture upon that Occasion.

Voted, That the Delegates of each perticular Association shall take an Attested Copy of all the Acts which are Passed in each perticular Session of the General Association, & deliver it to each perticular Association which sent them, to be Recorded or Kept on File. And that the Scribe of the General Association, after he has Entered the Acts of each Session in the Book, shall Convey the Book to the Place where the next General Association is Appointed to be Kept.

This Association having Read & Considered the Rev. Mr. Holmes'[s] Proposals respecting Ecclesiastical affairs, do Recommend the same to the Consideration of the several perticular Associations, & do Desire them to send their Opinion upon the said Proposals to the next General Association — Whether would be convenient for the Churches to come into some one or more of them.

A Question Proposed — Whether the Infant Slaves of Christian Masters may be Baptized in their Master's Right: Provided they Suitably Promise and Engage to bring them up in the Ways of Religion?

Resolved in the Affirmative.

Another Question Proposed — Whether it is the Duty of such Masters to offer such Children & to Promise as aforesaid? Resolved in the Affirmative.

Voted — that it be Recommended to the several perticular Associations to come into a Resolve, That every Candidate for the Ministry, shall pass the Examination & Approbation of the Association after he has had a Call to Settle in any perticular Place within their Bounds, & some suitable time before the Fast previous to the Ordination, & that no Minister shall assist in any Ordination without a Certificate That he has Passed such Examination & Approbation. Unless they have come into such a Resolve already.

Voted That the next General Association shall be at the Rev. Mr. Samuel Whittlesey's of Wallingford in the County of New Haven.

NOTES.

¹. Rev. William Burnham was pastor of the church in Kensington from 1712 to 1750. Mod^r in 1738 at Stratford.

². Rev. Jacob Hemingway was pastor of the church in East Haven from 1711 to 1754. Mod^r in 1743 at Fairfield.

³. Rev. Samuel Cook was pastor of the First Church in Bridgeport from 1715 to 1747.

⁴. Rev. Hezekiah Gold was pastor of the church in Stratford from 1720 to 1752.

⁵. Rev. Thomas Clap was pastor of the church in Windham from 1726 to 1739. He was called from this church to the Presidency of Yale College.

⁶. Rev. Thomas Ruggles was pastor of the First Church in Guilford from 1695 to 1728, & Rev. Thomas Ruggles Jr. from 1729 to 1770. Mod^r in 1766 at Guilford & 1767 at Mid^{own}.

⁷. Rev. Ashbel Woodbridge was pastor of the First Church in Glastenbury from 1728 to 1758.

⁸. Rev. Elnathan Whitman was pastor of the 2nd, or South Church in Hartford from 1733 to 1777. Mod^r in 1772 at Waterbury.

⁹. Rev. Ephraim Bostwick was pastor of the First Church in Greenwich from 1730 to 1746.

¹⁰. Rev. William Hart was pastor of the church in Saybrook from 1736 to 1783.

1740.

Att a Convention of the General Association of the Colony of Connecticut att Hartford June 17th 1740

Present —

The Rev.^{d}
- Mr. Tim Edwards Mod^r [1]
- Mr. Sam^{ll} Woodbridge [2]
- Mr. Isaac Stiles [3]
- Ashb^l Woodbridge, Scribe [4]
- Mr. Ephr^m Little [5]
- Mr. Jonath^n Parsons [6]
- Mr. Elisha Kent [7]
- Mr. Willm Gaylord [8]

Upon the consideration of ye Importance of Duly qualified Persons being recommended to Preach ye Gospel & put into ye Ministry, and ye dangerous consequence of ye contrary — Voted (for the present) To Recommend to Such particular Associations as do not practice them, the Rules for Examining Candidates for the Ministry agreed upon by ye General Association att their Convention att Fairfield Sept. 4th 1712.

Voted y^t for ye preventing of Such Disorders & Difficulties as have already arisen in Some of our Churches, or in case of neglects may hereafter arise — It be earnestly recommended to ye particular Associations that have not yet come into the practice To Keep close to ye Platform in calling Ecclesiastical Decisive Councils according to ye 7th Article of the same.

Voted y^t the next General Association be att ye Rev. Mr Solomon Williams's at Lebanon on ye 3^d Tuesday of June Next att 11 of ye clock A. M.

Notes.

[1]. Rev. Timothy Edwards was the pastor of the church in South Windsor from 1695 to 1755. He was the father of Jonathan Edwards, & married the daughter of the Rev. Solomon Stoddard. Mod^r in 1740 at Hartford.

[2]. Rev. Samuel Woodbridge was pastor of the church in East Hartford from 1705 to 1746.

[3]. Rev. Isaac Stiles was pastor of the church in North Haven from 1724 to 1760.

[4]. Rev. Ashbel Woodbridge was pastor of the church in Glastenbury from 1728 to 1758.

[5]. Rev. Ephraim Little was pastor of the church in Colchester from 1732 to 1787. He was Mod^r in 1763 at Lyme.

[6]. Rev. Jonathan Parsons was pastor of the church in Lyme, now Old Lyme, from 1730 to 1745.

[7]. Rev. Elisha Kent was pastor of the church in Newtown from 1732 to 1743.

[8]. Rev. William Gaylord was pastor of the church in Wilton from 1733 to 1765. He was Mod^r at Windham in 1751.

1741.

Att a Convention of the General Association of the Colony of Connecticut at Lebanon in the County of Windham on the 3ᵈ Tuesday of June 1741

Present

The Revᵈ.
1. Mr. Eleazer Williams, Modʳ
2. Mr. Stephen Steel
3. Mr. Solomon Williams
4. Mr. Thomas White
   Ephraim Little Scribe
5. Mr. George Beckwith
6. Mr. Jonathan Todd
7. Mr. Joseph Bellamy

This Association from what the particular members find among their own people, & from what they hear from Divers parts, being persuaded that there is great reason of thankfulness to God for an Extraordinary revival of religion in this Land, and being sensible of the great necessity of union, Zeal & Diligence in the ministry in order to further & carry on that great & good work, Voted to reccommend it to the particular Associations to keep up frequent Lectures in their respective parishes, and to interchange their Labors & help with one another for their mutual assistance and encouragement.

And it appearing to us of great Consequence to keep up & maintain a union in their Sentiments in the great Doctrines of Religion, in order to their living Charitably and with Brotherly affection and to prevent hard thoughts & hasty Censures one of another, Voted to Recommend it to the particular Associations to be very free to enform each other of their Sentiments in the great doctrines of Religion, and to endeavor to know whether they are in the same way of thinking on the Calvinissticall Doctrines and particularly on the Doctrine of Justification, and the nature of Conversion and Regeneration; and that they be free in Conversing together on Experimentall Religion and be agreed how far the Christian law of mutual forbearance and Charity ought to extend with respect to these matters. And 'tis desired that the thoughts of each particular Association and the nethod they shall come into the practice of hereupon, be communicated to the next General Association, in order to a union as far as possible on these heads.

Voted to be recommended to the particular Associations to take it into their Serious Consideration whether there ought not to be more weight laid upon the matters transmitted to them from the General Association than has been usually done heretofore, and whether if due Care was taken about these matters and in attendance upon the meetings of the General Association that might not be more useful and Servicable to the great end of its agreement or Constitution.

Voted that the next General Association be at the Rev^d Mr. Eliphalet Adam's at New London on the 3^d Tuesday of June next at eleven of the clock A.M., But if he cannot conveniently Receive it, that it be at the Rev^d. Mr. William Worthington's of Saybrook at the time afore said.

NOTES.

[1]. Pastor at Mansfield from 1710 to 1742.
[2].   "   at Tolland from 1722 to 1758.
[3].   "   at Lebanon from 1722 to 1776.
[4].   "   at Bolton from 1725 to 1763.
[5].   "   at Hamburg in Lyme from 1730 to 1772.
[6].   "   at East Guilford from 1733 to 1791.
[7].   "   at Bethlem from 1738 to 1789.

1742.

Att a Convention of the General Association of the Colony of Connecticutt at New London June 15: 1742

Present

The Rev. Messrs
1. Mr. Eliphalett Addams Moderator
2. Mr. Stephen Hosmer
3. Mr. Sam[ll] Dorrance
4. Mr. Benja[m] Colton Scribe
   Mr. Thomas Ruggles
5. Mr. Noah Hobart
6. Mr. Daniel Wadsworth
7. Mr. Theophilus Hall
   Mr. Ephraim Little

The Meeting was opened with Prayer.

This Gen[l] Association after humble addressing ourselves to God for his blessing upon us, and Direction to be given us in all our Consultations, Being of opinion that the God of all grace has been mercifully pleased to Remember and visit his people by Stiring up Great Numbers among us to a concern for their Souls, and to be asking the way to Zion with their faces thitherward, Which we desire to take notice of with Great Thankfulness to God the Father of Mercies.

Being also of the opinion that the great Enemy of Souls who is ever ready with his Devices to Check Damp & Destroy if possible the Work of God, is very busy for that purpose, We think it our duty to advise & Entreat the Ministers & Churches of the Colony, and recommend it to the Severall Associations to Stand well upon their guard in Such a day as this is That no detriment do arise to the interests of our great Lord & Master Jesus Christ —

Particularly that no Errors in Doctrine whether from among ourselves or foreigners, nor disorders in practice do get in among us, or tares be sown in the Lord's Field.

That seasonable and due testimony be borne against such

Errors & Irregularities as doe already prevail among some persons, As Particularly the Depending upon & following Impulses & impressions made on the mind as th'o they were immediate Revelations of Some truth, or Duty that is not Reveal[d] in the Word of God — Laying too much Weight upon bodily agitations, Raptures, Extacies, Visions &c — Ministers disorderly intruding into other Minister's parishes — Laymen taking it upon them in an unwarrantable manner publicly to teach and Exhort — Rash Censuring & Judging of others —

That the Elders be careful to take heed to themselves & Doctrine that they may save themselves and those that hear them; That they Approve themselves in all things as the Ministers of God, by Honor & dishonor, by good Report & evil Report, that none be Lifted up by applause to a vain conceit, nor any be cast down by any contempt thrown upon them to the neglect of their work: And that they study Unity, Love and peace among themselves. — And farther that they Endeavour to heal the unhappy Divisions that are already made in Some churches: and that the like may in the future be prevented.

That a just defference be paid to the laws of the Christian Magistrate: lately made for the Suppression of Disorder

That no countenance be given to such as trouble the Churches, who are according to the Constitution of our Churches under Censure, Suspension or Deposition, Whether for Errors in Doctrine or Life.

Humbly praying that our Great lord & Master, Jesus Christ who is head over all things to his Church will preserve it in purity & peace: That he will go on Conquoring & to Conquor Till not an Enemy to his Holy Truth & Ways shall be left among us, And that the Lord's Kingdom may come & his Will be done in Earth as it is in Heaven —

Voted that the next Meeting of the General Association be at Fairfield At the Rev. Mr. Noah Hobarts on the Third Tuesday of June next at Eleven a Clock Before Noon.

Unanimously voted by the association,

  Test Benja: Colton Scribe.

NOTES.

¹. Pastor 1ˢᵗ Church New London from 1708 to 1753.
². " 1ˢᵗ Church East Haddam from 1704 to 1749.
³. " at Voluntown & Sterling from 1723 to 1770.
⁴. " at West Hartford from 1713 to 1754.
⁵. " at Fairfield from 1733 to 1773.
⁶. " 1ˢᵗ Church Hartford from 1732 to 1747.
⁷. " 1ˢᵗ Church Meriden from 1729 to 1767.

1743.

Att a Convention of the Gen¹¹ Association of the Colony of Connecticutt att Fairfield June 21ˢᵗ 1743

Presᵗ —
  Mr. Jacob Hemingway Modʳ.
  Mr. Samˡˡ Cook
¹. Mr. William Russel Scribe
². Mr. William Worthington
The Revᵈ. ³. Mr. Moses Dickinson
⁴. Mr. Timothy Collins
  Mr. Thomas Ruggles
  Mr. Noah Hobart
  Mr. Ashbel Woodbridge.

The meeting was opened with Prayer. This General Association are of opinion that altho'; as it was observed by the Gen¹¹ Association Last year that God hath been pleased graciously to visit his people &c Yet thro' the Subtle Devices of Satan and the great Corruption there is in the hearts of men and the Enmity there is in them against Religion in the power & purity of it, there are diverse things w.ᶜʰ have a threat'ning aspect on the Interest of Religion in Gen¹¹ in the Land and in this Government in perticular for the Removing and preventing of which we Recommend it to the particular Associations that they be very careful

1. that the true and great Doctrines of the Gospel agreeable to our Confession of faith be maintained & preacht up,

against the Arminian Antinomian and other errors: and that special Care & pains be taken with our youth to Instruct them in the principles of our holy Religion and articles of our faith.

2. to maintain the credit of the ordinances of the Gospel Especially the word of God contained in the holy Scriptures as the outward and ordinary means of Salvation.

3. to maintain the order & Government that Christ hath Established in his visible C'h, and that they do not countenance any breaking in upon it: By persons Departing from or neglecting the Worship and Communion of the assemblies and churches to which they belong on a supposition of the ministers or many of the members being unconverted, or in cold dead frames

or by ministers and churches Receiving to Communion those that are under Censure in the Churches to which they belong, .

or by ministers going into other minister's parishes and preaching or administering the Seals contrary to the mind of the settled minister of the place

But that they preserve a steady discipline and bear a proper testimony against all imorallities and Impieties yet with such patience & meekness as the nature and circumstances of the cases Require.

And we would Recomend it to our Brethren in the ministry as of great importance to the advancement of the Interest of Christ that they take heed to themselves that they be examples to their flocks in all holy cenversation and godliness.

Voted.

Voted that the next annual meeting of the Gen[11] association be at the Rev. Mr. Chauncy's of Durham on the third tuesday of June next at eleven of the clock beforenoon.

Notes.

[1]. Pastor 1st Middletown from 1715 to 1761.
[2].   "   Westbrook from 1726 to 1756.
[3].   "   Norwalk from 1727 to 1765.
[4].   "   1st Litchfield from 1723 to 1752.

1744.

Att a Convention of the Gen[l] Association of the Colony of Connecticutt att Durham June 19: 1744

Pres[t]

     1. Mr. Nathaniel Chauncey Mod[r]
     2. Mr. Jared Eliot
     Mr. William Russell Scribe
     Mr. Benjamin Colton
The Rev[d] 3. Mr. Sam[ll] Hall
     4. Mr. John Goodsell
     5. Mr. Simon Backus
     Mr. Daniel Wadsworth
     Mr. George Beckwith
     6. Mr. Ebenezer Devotion

The Convention was open'd w'th prayer and the following Resolves and Conclusions were unanimously come into.

Viz: 1. That — Whereas at all times but more Especially at this time Sundry persons Unjustly disaffected to and prejudiced against Either the minister or Ch; or both to which they belong under the Influence of Such disaffection withdraw from their worship & Comunion; and allthough as yet they are under no Censure, Yet we think that other ministers & Ch[s] receiving such disaffected persons to privileges Serves to Incourage and Strengthen them in their unjust disaffection & unreasonable Separation w'ch to prevent it may be proper that the minister by himself or in Conjunction with some of the Brethren of such C'h from wh[ch] there is such separation Write to the minister or ministers of such C'h or Ch[s] to w'h the afores'[d] disaffected members repair for privileges and in a Brotherly & kind manner represent to them the true State of Such members & Ch[s] desiring them to discountenance & prevent Such Separations, and in case a minister or ministers so Informed and applied to shall still receive & incourage such persons that then the

Complainant Lay the matter before the Association to w'ch that minister doth belong that so the Association deal wth him as the nature and circumstances of the case doth require. And Inasmuch as we Judge that such Separations countenanced as aboves[d] is the source and original of much difficulty and a practice big wth many mischiefs we earnestly recomend the affair to the perticular Associations that in this or some other way they provide against so great an evil that may be by divine blessing soon & easily prevented or cured. And that ministers should be very cautious of entertaining such dissaffected persons & of hearing & countenancing their reports of or against their ministers & Ch[s].

2. Whither a minister or a number of ministers Entring into any Established parish in this Government & there Gathering a C[h] of members that had before disorderly separated themselves from the C[h] to w[ch] they belonged, and some of them actually under Ecclesiastical censure, be not matter of offence.

Voted in the Affirmative

3. Whither to require persons perticularly to promise to walk in comunion wth this Ch of Christ into w'ch they Seek admission conscienciously attending and up holding the Public worship of God in this place till regularly dismis[t] therefrom be a hard or unreasonable term of Comunion.

Resolve in the negative.

And we think it not Advisable to admit a person to Comunion that refuses to Submit to the abovementioned terms.

But Insists on being at Liberty to go to other places when and where he pleases to attend the public worship & ordinances

4. Whither Males in full Comunion being under the age of 21 years have right to vote in C'h affairs?

Voted that this question be refer'd to the perticular Associations for their Resolves upon it, to be sent in to the next Gen[ll] Association.

Voted that the next Gen[ll] Association be at Newington in the County of Hartford at the Rev.[d] Mr. Backus's on the third Tuesday of June next at eleven of the clock in the forenoon.

NOTES.

1. Pastor 1ˢᵗ Durham from 1711 to 1756.
2. " Clinton from 1709 to 1763.
3. " Cheshire from 1724 to 1776.
4. " Greenfield from 1726 to 1756.
5. " Newington from 1725 to 1745.
6. " Scotland from 1735 to 1771.

1745.

Att a Convention of the General Association of the Colony of Connecticut at Newington in the County of Hartford on the 18th Day of June 1745

Present

The Rev.ᵈ
1. Mr. Benjamin Colton, Modʳ
   Mr. Abraham Nott.
2. Mr. Jacob Eliot.
   Mr. Ashbel Woodbridge.
   Mr. Simon Bacchus.
3. Elnathan Whitman, Scribe
   Mr. William Gaylord.
4. Mr. Ephraim Avery.

The Meeting was opened with Prayer and the following Resolves were come into.

Whereas there has of late years been many Errors in Doctrine, and Disorders in Practice, prevailing in the Churches of this Land, which seem to have a threatening aspect upon these Churches; and whereas Mr. George Whitefield has been the Promoter, or at least the Faulty occasion of many of these Errors and Disorders, this Association think it needfull for them to declare that if the said Mr. Whitefield should make his progress thro' this Government, it would by no means be advisable for any of our Ministers to admitt him into their Pulpits, or for any of our people to attend upon his Preaching and Administrations.

Voted in the affirmative.

This Association apprehending that Ecclesiastical Discipline has been greatly neglected in our Churches and that the Revival of it, & keeping of it up, is of great Importance to the Welfare of the Churches, would Recommend it to the several particular Associations to consider whether it be not Needful for them to Endeavour to revive and keep up a strict discipline in our Churches according to the Order of the Gospel.

Voted by this Association that it be recommended to the several particular Associations to consider whether it may not be a good expedient to prevent Difficulty in the Management of Discipline in our Churches, that whenever any of the Members of our Churches remove their habitation from one Town or Parish to another, that they be actually dismissed or recommended from the Church from which they remove, in Order to their being taken under the Care and Watch of the Church to which they remove.

Voted that the next General Association be at the Rev[d] Mr. Jacob Eliot's at Goshen in Lebanon, on the third Tuesday of June next at eleven of the clock in the forenoon.

Notes.

[1]. Pastor at Centerbrook from 1725 to 1756.
[2]. " Goshen, Lebanon from 1729 to 1766.
[3]. " 2nd Hartford from 1733 to 1767.
[4]. " Brooklyn, Pomfret from 1735 to 1754.

1746.

Att a Convention of the Association of the Colony of Connecticut at Goshen in Lebanon on the 3ᵈ Tuesday of June 1746

Present —

The Revᵈ
¹. Mr. Henry Willes
Mr. Stephen Steel Modʳ
Mr. Jacob Eliott
Mr. Thomas White
Mr. Isaac Stiles
². Mr. Marston Cabott
Ephraim Little Scribe
Mr. William Gaylord
³. Mr. Benjamin Woodbridge

This Convention was opened by prayer and the following Resolves were unanimously come into viz:

That it be recommended by this Association to the Several particular Associations in the Colony to consider whether it is not a very proper thing for the Ministers of this Government unitedly to make a Sutable Address to his Majesty, our rightfull Sovereign King George on the occasion of the present war — the Rebellion at home, the Success of his Majestie's Arms in the reduction of Cape Britton, and elsewhere, as well as on the expedition against Canada.

It was proposed, whether the pretence of better Edification be sufficient to Justify persons in their withdrawing from a Particular church to which they belong; either from the Communion or public worship of the Same, or both, and for their attending either Statedly in other Churches where they pretend they can be better edified.

Resolved in the Negative.

The Rev. Mr. Henry Willes pastor of the 2ⁿᵈ Church of Christ in Norwich represented to us the State of the Church with them, That a long time hath passed since the Sacrament of the Lord's Supper was administered, and that he the s[d] Mr. Willes & brethren attending his ministry, having pursued all measures that have been prescribed to them by the last Council to accomodate their differences, and desiring our advise whether it be Convenient for him to administer the Sacrament of the Lord's Supper to those of his Church that are meet & willing Communicants,

Voted in the Affirmative, and according advised that the Rev. Mr. Willes administer the Sacrament of the holy Supper.

The question was put whether a Complaint by any member or members of a Church against a Number of the Same Church (th'o y[e] Major part of s[d] church of which the Complainant or complainants are Members) for Scandalous violation or violations of any rule or rules of God's word, may and ought to be exhibited to the Pastor of s[d] Church in order to be communicated for their Consideration & determination?

Voted in the Affirmative.

It was proposed whether the Persons complained of as afores'd ought to be allowed y[e] priviledge of voting in their own Case in any Church-meeting at which they are Called to an account for their misconduct?

Voted in the Negative.

Voted that the next meeting of the General Association be at the Rev.[d] Mr. William Worthington's of Saybrook, if he is willing to receive it — otherwise that it be at the Rev. Mr. William Hart's in Saybrook afores[d], on the 3rd Tuesday of June next at Eleven of the clock in the forenoon.

NOTES.

[1]. Pastor in Franklin   from 1718 to 1753.
[2].   "   "   Thompson   "   1730 to 1756.
[3].   "   "   Woodbridge "   1742 to 1783.

1747.

Att a meeting of y⁰ General Association of y⁰ Colony of Connecticut at Saybrook, West Parish, in y⁰ County of New-London June 16: A. D. 1747

Present

The Rev. Mess⁰.
1. Jared Eliott Mod'.
   Wil^m Worthington
2. Jonathan Merick Scribe
3. Isaac Chalker
   Jonathan Todd
   Ephraim Avery
4. Gideon Mills
5. James Cogswell

The Convention was opened with prayer, and ye Ques^n being put, whether it be agreeable to Gospel order for ye members of particular Chh^s to attend upon ye Sacriment in ye chh or chh's to which they belong, Generally at other times to worship in other Societies although regular and Established —

This Case as to Substance hath been resolved already, by ye General Association June 19 A. D. 1744, as may be seen by the records of ye s^d Association — and we think that Those persons are offenders and to be Dealt with as Such, who although yy attend ye Sacriment in ye chh or chh's to which yy Belong yet at other times make a Practice of withdrawing from ye worship of ye Same, Excepting the Circumstances of Cituation do make it more convenient to attend ye Divine worship else where; and even in that Case we think it Disorderly to withdraw as affore^sd, without the Consent of ye Church.

Whereas we understand y^t ye Book of Discipline and Confession of faith agreed upon at Saybrook are Scarce in our Chhs, and that ye Secretary hath a Number of y^m in his Custody (which is at his Dispose) we desire ye Rev. Mr.

Chalker of Easbury in yᵉ name of this Association to apply to him for, receive and divide yᵉ same in yᵉ several Counties in this Colony, and send yᵐ as soon as may be, and we think it advisable that one of sᵈ books do always accompany yᵉ Book of records of yᵉ several Associations, That it may be always present in yᵉ respective Conventions to be used upon occasion,

Voted that yᵉ next Meeting of yᵉ Genˡˡ Association be at yᵉ Rev. John Goodell's at Fairfield if he is willing to receive it, otherwise that it be at yᵉ Rev. Mr. Hunn's at Reading on yᵉ 3ʳᵈ Tusday of June next at eleven of yᵉ clock in yᵉ fore-noon.

NOTES.

¹. Pastor in Westbrook from 1726 to 1756.
². " North Brandford from 1716 to 1769.
³. " East Glastonbury from 1744 to 1765.
⁴. " Simsbury from 1744 to 1754.
⁵. " Canterbury from 1744 to 1771 &
    " Scotland from 1772 to 1804.

1748.

At a Convention of the General Association of the Colony of Connecticut at Reading in the County of Fairfield June 21, 1748

Present

Mr. Benjamin Colton Mod.ʳ
Mr. Noah Hobart
Mr. John Goodsel
¹. Sam.ˡ Whittlesey jun, Scribe
The Rev.ᵈ ². Mr. Moses Bartlett
³. Mr. Nathaniel Hunn
⁴. Mr. Hezekiah Bissell
Mr. Joseph Bellamy
⁵. Mr. Nathan Birdsey

The Moderator opened the meeting with prayer.

This Association taking into Serious Consideration the great importance of instructing Children in their most early years in the Principles of Christianity, and observing that altho' the Assemblies Shorter Catechism be a most excellent Summary of the Christian Religion, and what we would by no means have laid aside or disused, yet think that some plain & easy Introduction to it to be learned by Children before they are of a suitable age to enter upon that Catechism might be of great advantage, would earnestly recommend to our people the use of the Rev.^{d} Dr. Watts's excellent Setts of Catechisms and think that a new edition of them would be of great Service. In the use of those Catechisms we would recommend it to Parents to begin with the first of them as soon as their Children are capable of learning it, which will naturally bring them to enter upon the Assemblies Catechism at the proper age for using it to advantage; and if the particular associations would agree to Encourage and forward one another in introducing this method of catechizing in their several Congregations we think it might be an happy means of promoting Religion among us.

This association understanding that the Confession of Faith and Articles of Chh Discipline agreed upon at Saybrook are very scarce in our Churches, and that a number of said Books are in the hands of the Secretary to be disposed of, & finding that the last General Association had desired the Rev.^{d} Mr. Chalker of Eastbury to apply to the Secretary for them & distribute them in the Several Counties, but not having heard that Mr. Chalker hath so done, we desire the Rev.^{d} Mr. Colton & the Rev.^{d} Mr. Whitman of Hartford to undertake that affair; and if there be not a sufficiency found with the Secretary we desire said Gentlemen to Present to the Gen^{ll} Assembly at their next Sessions the great want of these Books, and move for a new edition.

This Association Observing the great prevalence of vice & prophaneness, and a Lamentable Indifference in Spiritual Concerns among our people, & having Seriously considered what likely method can be taken to awaken our people & Revive a spirit of Seriousness and practical Religion among us, are of opinion that for Ministers in their Several parishes to take frequent Opportunies & Discourse in private with particular persons upon Religious & eternal things, & to make a personal Address to them, would have a happy tendency to beget a Spirit of Seriousness, and to Revive true Religion among us, do therefore earnestly recommend it to our Several Associations to Encourage & promote such a practice among them.

Voted that the next meeting of the Gen.[1] Association be at the House of the Rev.[d] Mr. Joseph Noyes of New Haven, on the 3rd Tuesday of June next at eleven o'clock A. M.

Test SAM[ll] WHITTLESEY Jun. Scribe

NOTES.

[1]. Pastor in Wallingford from 1709 to 1752.
[2]. " 1st Portland from 1733 to 1766.
[3]. " Redding from 1733 to 1749.
[4]. " Bloomfield from 1738 to 1783.
[5]. " West Haven from 1742 to 1758.

1749.

There were so few Delegates came to the Gen[ll] Association appointed to be at the Rev. Mr. Noyes's of New Haven the third Tuesday of June 1749 that t'was thought not best to enter on any business; Only to appoint the next Gen[ll] Ass.[n] to be at Hartford at the house of the Rev.[d] Mr. Benjamin Colton on the third Tuesday of June next at Eleven of the Clock A. M. and to Notifie the Several Ass. that had not Delegates pr's't, this I was Desir'd to Enter in the Ass. Book.

New Haven June 20, 1749

WILLIAM RUSSELL

1750.

Att a Convention of the General Association of the Colony of Connecticut In West Hartford June 19, 1750

Present

  Mr. William Russell, Moderator
  Mr. Benjamin Colton
The Rev⁴. Mr. Stephen Steal
  Mr. William Gaylord
  Mr. John Trumble Scribe [1]

This Association finding of it Enter'd In our Book that there were so few members of the General association met the Last year att the Rev^d. Mr. Joseph Noyes's att New Haven that the Gentlemen did not think it Prudent to enter upon Business. And now there being so few Present; we were in Suspence whether It was best for us to form Into an association, yet at length concluded that we would — and Do hereby Inform the Perticular associations that if this association is so Thinly attended by reason of Sickness or the Like; we Look upon it a sore frown of Providence. But if it's thro Negligence or Carelessness we suppose that it argues too Little Regard to the Constitution and would Intreat of Every Perticular association that they would by no means omit appointing of Delegates from time to time; and that Those Gentlemen that are so appointed would be Careful to attend accordingly; that so the good Ends Proposed In the meetings may not be wholy frustrate and disapointed.

Voted that the Next meeting of the General association be att the house of the Rev. Mr. Stephen Whites of Windham on the 3^d Tuesday of June Next att Eleven o'clock A.M.

        Test JOHN TRUMBLE Scribe.

NOTES.

[1]. Pastor at Watertown from 1739 to 1784.

1751.

At a Convention of the General Association of the Colony of Connecticutt at Windham in the County of Windham June 18: 1751

Present

The Revd Messrs {
1. Daniel Fuller
   William Gaylord
   Ebenezer Devotion
2. Benjamin Pomroy
3. Stephen White
4. Noah Welles
5. Edward Dorr.
}

Mr. Gaylord was chosen Moderator, and Mr. Welles Scribe. Prayer was attended by the Moderator.

A motion being made in this Association that an Address of Condolence be presented to his Majesty, and another to the Princess of Wales, in the Name of the General Association, upon the Mournful Occasion of the late Death of his Royal Highness Frederick, Prince of Wales, and accordingly an Address in each case being laid before the Association for their Consideration, after particular Examination and some few Corrections it was Unanimously voted that said Addresses be forthwith Offered as soon as opportunity presents.

Voted that said Addresses be inclosed in a Letter to Benjamin Avery Esqr. of London Doctor of Laws with a desire in the Name of this Assoc^n that he would be pleas'^{d} to present s'^{d} Addresses accordingly.

Voted that Mr. Devotion and Mr. White transcribe ye said Addresses, and forward them by the first Opportunity inclos'd in a Letter to Doct^r Avery in the Name of the Moderator.

The Association recommend it to the Several Associations within the Colony, to prepare, each Association, a Draught, and send it by their Respective Delegates to the next General Assoc^n, out of which they may draw a Plan to be first sent to the Several Consociations for their approbation, which being Obtained, to be prefer'd to the Hon'e General Assembly for their Sanction upon it — which Plan to Contain in it —

1. This addition to the present Ecclesiastical Constitution of Gov.[1] viz: that there be a General Consociation of Ministers and Churches, Two ministers and two Messengers from each Consociation to make up said General Consociation, To which there may be appeals from the Judgment of particular Consociations.

2. This alteration in it, that there shall be no Vote in any Consociation within the Establishment, without a Majority both of Elders and Messengers present in it.

3. That in Ordinary cases, no Complaint shall be in the Church or Consociation against any Church Member, for a Crime committed, So long before Process that the Civil Court would reject it, or does refuse a Process, merely upon account of the age of the Crime complain'd of.

It is Judged advisable by this Assoc[n] that there be for the Future, a General Convention of the Ministers of this Colony at New Haven the Day after the Commencement annually, at which time Some Minister by previous appointment shall deliver Concionem ad Clerum and that the said appointment of the Preacher be for the future made at ye annual Convention, and accordingly we agree to Desire the Rev.^{d} Mr. Whittlesey of Wallingford to preach the Convention Sermon at the first Convention on Septr Next and in case of his failure, that the Rev. Mr. Hobart of Fairfield be Desired to preach on s^d Occasion.

Voted That the next Meeting of the General Ass[n] on the 3rd Tuesday of June next, be at Mr. Eliot's of Killingworth.

Test NOAH WELLES Scribe

NOTES.

[1]. Pastor in Willington from 1728 to 1758.
[2]. " in Hebron from 1735 to 1784.
[3]. " Windham from 1740 to 1793.
[4]. " Stamford from 1746 to 1776.
[5]. " 1st Hartford from 1748 to 1772.

1752.

At a Convention of the Gen[ll] Association of the Colony of Connecticut, at Killingworth in the County of New London June 16: 1752

Present

Jared Elliot
Thomas Ruggles
John Goodsell
[1]. Joseph Fish
The Rev[d] Mess[s] William Hart
Jonathan Todd
[2]. Edward Eells
[3]. Moses Mather

The Rev[d] Mr Jared Elliot was chosen Mod[r], Thomas Ruggles was chosen Scribe. The Convention was opened with prayer by the Mod[tr].

Whereas the Gen[ll] Association at their last Convention did Recommend to the Several particular Associations That Some Scheme be proposed by them for the Forming a Gen[ll] Consociation, And that the Respective Associations should Transmit their opinions thereupon to this Convention.

But the Particular Associations not having so done, voted That s[d] Affair be Referred to the next Meeting of the Gen[ll] Association; And that the Respective Associations who have not Signified their opinions thereupon be Earnestly Desired, seriously to Deliberate upon the subject; and send their Advice thereupon to s[d] meeting.

Voted that it be Strenuously Recommended to the particular Associations that they be Desired to take more effectual care with Respect to their members who are to attend upon the Gen[ll] Association; Both in choosing them and that they Punctually and Faithfully Attend upon the Meeting; That So the wise and good end of that part of our Constitution may be fully Answered.

And to Render the Convention of the Gen'l Association more extensively useful It be Recommended; That such Questions of Importance as may arise upon Reading or Study by particular persons, Or may So Do in the management of Public Affairs in the Churches: Be proposed First to the particular Associations where they do arise to be answered by them: And then that they be transferred by that association, to the Gen'l Association with Their opinion or Resolution Thereupon; s'd Questions to be Casuistically and Critically Considered & Resolved as a proper method & means to promote & Encrease the careful Study of the Holy Scriptures as well as Satisfaction of such who Labor under Doubts or Difficulties therein. S'd Questions & Resolutions when Satisfactorily Answered, either by the particular Association to which they are first proposed, or by the Gen'l Association to be entred by the Scribe in the Records of the Gen'l Association.

Voted that the next Meeting of the Gen'l Association be Holden on the Third Tuesday of June next ensuing in Fairfield County, At the House of the Rev'd Mr. Goodsell's, at eleven o'Clock before noon — and that in case any thing should intervene that it cannot be conveniently attended at s'd place: Then that it meet at the Rev'd Mr. Buckingham's in the West Parish of Fairfield.

Test THOMAS RUGGLES Scribe

A true Record, Test THOMAS RUGGLES Scribe.

NOTES.

1. Pastor in No. Stonington - from 1732 to 1781.
2. " Cromwell - - from 1738 to 1776.
3. " in Darien - - - from 1744 to 1806.

1753.

At a Convention of the Gen[l] Association of the Colony of Connecticut at the west parish of Fairfield in the County of Fairfield June 19: 1753

Present —

The Rev.[d] Mess.[s]
{ Noah Hobart
Elnathan Whitman
Ephraim Little
Samuel Whittelsey
Daniel Buckingham '.
Nathan Birdsey
Samuel Newell   ².
Joseph Fowler   ³.
James Beebee   ⁴.
Izrahiah Wetmore   ⁵. }

The Rev.[d] Mr. Noah Hobart was chosen Moderator — and Samuel Whittlesey Scribe. The Convention was opened with prayer by the Moderator.

A former Gen[l] Association having Judged it adviseable that there be a Gen[l] Convention of the ministers of this Colony annually at New Haven the day after Commencement, and that a *Conscio ad Clerum* be delivered on that Occasion by some minister previously appointed; but the affair having not yet been carried into Execution — This association highly approving of the Design do propose and Recommend that such a Convention be attended the day after the next Commencement, and Request the Rev[d] Mr. Hobart of Fairfield and in case of his failure the Rev.[d] Mr. Whitman of Hartford to preach the Sermon on that Occasion at 10 o'clock of said day.

The Gen[l] Association having formerly recommended it to the particular associations of this Colony to draw up a Scheme for the forming a General Consociation for the receiving appeals from particular associations, but several particular associations not having sent in any Scheme for this purpose to the General Association; we still recommend it to those associations that have not yet Signified their thoughts upon this affair, that they would prepare Draughts to be sent in to the next Gen[ll] Association, that out of the Several Draughts sent in to the Gen[ll] Association they may draw up a Scheme for Executing this Design — and it is further desired by this association that the Gen[ll] Convention of the Ministers which is Expected to meet at New Haven the day after the next Commencement would take this affair of a Gen[ll] Consociation into Consideration.

Voted that the next Meeting of the Gen.[ll] association be at the house of the Rev.[d] Mr. Hall of N. Cheshire on the 3rd Tuesday of June next at 11 o'clock.

Test. Sam[ll] Whittelsey, Scribe.

Notes.

[1]. Pastor at Greens' Farms from 1742 to 1766.
[2]. " Bristol from 1747 to 1789.
[3]. " East Haddam 1751 to 1771.
[4]. " Trumbull 1747 to 1785.
[5]. " Stratford 1753 to 1780.

1754.

At a Convention of the General Association of the Colony of Connecticut at New Cheshire in Wallingford in the County of New Haven y[e] 18th June 1754

Present

The Rev[d] Mess[rs]
- Samuel Hall
- William Worthington
- Abraham Nott
- Andrew Bartholomew [1].
- Benjamin Strong [2].
- Jonathan Ingersol [3].
- Nathan Birdsey
- John Norton [4].
- Samuel Newel
- Cyrus Marsh [5].
- Timothy Pitkin [6].

The Rev^d Mr. Samuel Hall was chosen Mod^r — Timothy Pitkin Chosen Scribe. The Convention was opened with Prayer by the Mod^r.

The General association having frequently recommended to the Several Particular Associations in this Colony to draw up a Scheme for the forming a General Consociation, for the Receiving and hearing appeals from particular Consociations; there has been a Scheme or Draught sent in for this purpose to the general association, from some particular associations, but since notwithstanding frequent Recommendations Several particular associations have not Sent a Scheme according to Desire and for afores^d purpose, We do still earnestly recommend it to the Several particular associations that have not yet Sent, that they wo'd Signifie their thots in this matter and wo'd prepare and send in their Draught and Scheme to the next Gen^ll association, that from these Schemes and Draughts there may be Collected and Concerted a Scheme by the General association for the Promoting and Executing this Design. And the New recommendation is to these Particular associations viz: to the association in Hartford County north and south Districts; to the association in the County of Litchfield; to the association in the Eastern Circuit in Fairfield County, the association in the County of New London.

Adjourned till the next morning Seven o'clock June 19: 1754. Convened according to adjournment. *Voted* that the next Meeting of the General Association be held at the house of the Rev. Mr. Eells in Middletown on the third tuesday of June next at Eleven o'clock A. M.

Test TIMOTHY PITKIN Scribe.

NOTES.

1. Pastor at Harwinton from 1738 to 1774.
2. " Stanwich from 1735 to 1763.
3. " Ridgefield from 1740 to 1778.
4. " East Hampton from 1748 to 1778.
5. " Kent from 1741 to 1755.
6. " Farmington from 1752 to 1785.

1755.

At a General Association of the Colony of Connecticut, at the Rev. Mr. Eelles's in the North Society in Middletown June 17, 1755

Present—

The Rev^d. Messrs {
Jared Eliot
Benjⁿ Colton
John Graham¹.
Willm Worthington
Solomon Williams
Jacob Eliot
Noah Hobart
Elnathan Whitman
Nathaniel Eelles ².
Jonathⁿ Todd
Edward Eelles
Jos: Bellamy
Noah Welles
James Bebee
Izrahiah Wetmore
}

Mr. Jared Eliot was chosen Moderator and Mr. Welles Scribe.

The Meeting was opened with Prayer by ye Moderator.

This Association apprehending, that various Errors contrary to ye Doctrines owned in the Churches of this Colony, are spreading and prevailing in the Land; and that it is highly necessary for Ministers to bear a Testimony against those preaching Errors; this Association would earnestly recommend it to the particular Associations of this Colony, to agree among themselves, frequently to insist upon those Doctrines contained in our Confession of Faith, which are contrary to the prevailing Errors of the Day: and particularly that they would bear a seasonable Testimony against Socinianism, Arrianism, Arminianism, Pelagianism and Antinomianism, or any other Errors that may arise among us.

And whereas one particular Association of the Colony have declined coming into the Proposal of a Gen[ll] Consociation till the Several Associations have declared their adherance to the Confession of Faith owned in our Churches; we freely declare our adherance to the Doctrines contained in our Confession of Faith and we would recommend it to particular Associations strictly to adhere to the Doctrines of our Confession of Faith.

The Association adjourn'[d] till 6 o'clo[ck] tomorrow Morning.

June 18 Met according to adjournment. Wheras most of the particular Associations in this Colony, have sent in to this Bord their Express Approbation of the Motion formerly made, that there should be a *Concio ad Clerum* at New Haven the Day after the Public Commencement, annually, and their Desire that said Practice should be continued; This Association taking the Affair into Consideration, unanimously approve of and concur with said Motion and Desire. And for the more effectual carrying into Execution the Purpose and Design aforesaid, recommend it as our Opinion and Advice, that it be referred to y[e] particular Associations to appoint the Preacher for that Occasion from Time to Time for the Future. And forasmuch as there is an appointment already made for the next Commencement, after which the advice aforesaid is to take Place; we recommend that the future appointments of the several particular associations be in Manner and Order following viz: in Fairfield Western Association. In the Eastern Association in said County. The County of New Haven. The South Association in the County of Hartford. The North Association in said County. In y[e] County of Windham. The Western Association in the County of N. London. The Eastern Association in s[d] County. The Association in the County of Litchfield.

This Association apprehending that there is danger of some bad Consequences arising from the Common Method of Licenceing candidates for the Ministry without any Limitation as to Time, recommend it to the Particular Associations to come into agreement to limit the Licence of Candidates to the Term of four Years, with these Exceptions viz: That such Limitations shall not respect Preachers that have been Ordained Ministers; nor Candidates preaching upon Probation and under Call to settle with that People to whom they are preaching; nor such Candidates as are necessarily hindered from attending the next Association after the Expiration of four years.

This Association taking into Consideration the Importance of having a Professor of Divinity in Yale College would recommend it to the several Ministers in the Colony to forward and promote among their People the Subscription set on foot for promoting that Design. And in the mean Time, in consideration of the great Burden that lies on the Rev^d the President, while he supplies the Place of a Professor; we recommend it to the Neighboring Ministers to assist him by Preaching occasionally in the College Hall.

Ordered that the next Gen[ll] Association of this Colony be holden at the House of the Rev^d Mr. Devotion of Windham, on the third Tuesday of June next.

The Rev. Mess^s Worthington and Todd declar'^{d} before the Association that whereas they are uncertain as to the Design and Business of a Professor of Divinity in this College, and have some scruples as to the Regularity of the Meeting of the Scholars in the Hall for Public Worship they therefore Dissent from the Vote of the Association respecting the same, and Desire their Dissent may be recorded.

After which the Session was closed with the Prayer of the Moderator. The above Voted as the Doings of this Association. Test NOAH WELLES Scribe.

NOTES.

[1]. Pastor at West Suffield from 1746 to 1792.
[2]. " Stonington from 1733 to 1786.

1756.

At a Meeting of the General Association of the Colony of Connecticut holden at the House of the Rev.ᵈ Mr. Ebenezar Devotion in Windham June 15 : 1756

Present.

The Rev.ᵈ Messrs
- George Griswold [1].
- Solomon Williams
- Elnathan Whitman
- Grindal Rawson [2].
- George Beckwith
- Ebenezar Devotion
- Hezekiah Bissell
- Hobart Estabrook [3].
- David Judson [4].
- Mark Levinworth [5].
- Moses Mather
- Asher Rosseter [6]
- Nathaniel Bartlett [7].

The Rev.ᵈ Mr. Solomon Williams was chosen Moderator and Elnathan Whitman was chosen Scribe.

The meeting was opened with Prayer by the Moderator.

This Association apprehending that there is Need of a New Impression of the Confession of Faith owned in the Churches of this Colony and of the Rules of Discipline established by the laws of this Colony, recommend it to particular Associations to promote a Subscription among their People for the reprinting sᵈ Book as soon as may be, and it is the Desire of this Association that what Subscriptions may be obtained by the Ministers, belonging to the several Associations, might be sent to the Rev. Mr. George Beckwith, and that he would enquire of the Printer, what sᵈ Book may be printed for, and that if a sufficient Number be subscribed for that the sᵈ Mr. Beckwith would agree with some Printer to print sᵈ Book, and correct the Press, and this Association desire their own Members immediately to set on Foot a Subscription for reprinting s^d Book.

The last General Association having recommended it to particular Associations to adhere to the Doctrines contained in the Confession of Faith owned in our Churches; this Association would further recommend it, to those particular Associations that have not declared their Concurrence with s^d Confession of Faith, to declare their Concurrence with it, and certify it to the next General Association.

The following Questions were proposed and Resolved.

¹. Quest. Whether the licensing a Candidate for Preaching vests him with any proper Office, or makes him a proper Officer in the Church? *Resolved* in the Negative.

². Quest. Whether such License be anything more than an orderly Leave (being given upon examination) to preach for a time, and that in order to a Judgment's being further made by Ministers and Churches, whether he have those Qualifications necessary to be found in a Gospel Minister?

Resolved that such License is nothing more than such a limited License for this end.

³. Whether those that give such Leave, or License, have not equal Power or Right, to recall the same, upon their judging it expedient and necessary so to do?

Resolved in the Affirmative.

This Association recommend it to the particular Associations in this Colony to make a Draught of some Emendations in our Rules of Ecclesiastical Discipline more especially with Respect to the Manner of Voting in Councils of the Consociation, which Draughts should be sent to the next General Association for them to draw something out of, that may be to the Acceptance of the Churches.

In consideration of the threatening Aspect of divine Providence at this day, particularly in the frequent and amazing Earthquakes, and their terrible Effects in various parts of the Earth, and Especially the strange, unusual and distressing War that is prevailing in this Land, as also in Consideration of the awful Growth and Spread of Vice and Immorality, this Association think it advisable that some time should be spent in humble and earnest Prayer and Supplication to God, to avert the Token of his Displeasure and save us from Sin and from Ruin, and especially that he would protect, defend and succeed our Armies in their present Expedition; and accordingly we recommend it to the several Ministers in the Colony (before the day of Prayer that may be appointed by Authority) to agree with their People to spend some time in Prayer every last Thursday in the Month for several Months next coming for the End afores'd, unless where Ministers and their People have already come into some different agreement; at which Times we think it best to be left discretionary whether to spend the whole Time in Prayer, or that the Minister if he be able, give the people a sermon suitable to the Occasion.

Voted that the next General Association shall be at the House of the Rev. Mr. Nathaniel Eells in Stonington on the Third Tuesday of June next, at Eleven of the clock in the Forenoon.

The above was voted as the doings of this Association.

Test, ELNATHAN WHITMAN, Scribe

after which the Sessions was closed with Prayer.

NOTES.

[1]. George Griswold Pastor in East Lyme from 1724 to 1761.
[2]. Grindal Rawson " Hadlyme from 1745 to 1777.
[3]. Hobart Estabrook " Millington from 1745 to 1766.
[4]. David Judson " Newtown from 1743 to 1776.
[5]. Mark Levinworth " Waterbury from 1740 to 1795.
[6]. Asher Rosseter " Preston from 1744 to 1781.
[7]. Nathaniel Bartlett " Redding from 1753 to 1810.

1757.

At a Gen'l Association of the Colony of Connecticut at the House of the Rev'd Mr. Nathaniel Eells in the East Society of Stonington June 21ˢᵗ 1757

Present

The Rev. 'Messᵉˢ
- Jacob Eliot
- Daniel Fuller
- Jonathan Merrick¹.
- Nathaniel Eells
- Joseph Fish
- George Beckwith
- Ebenezer Devotion
- Jonathan Todd
- Edward Eells
- Benjamin Throop².
- John Norton
- Elijah Sill³.

The Rev. Mr. Jacob Eliot was chosen Moderator & Messʳˢ Joseph Fish & Ebenʳ Devotion Scribes —

The meeting being opened with Prayer by the Modʳ & a Letter Drawn by the Rev. Mr. Ebenʳ Devotion to Doctʳ Benjamin Avery in London, in vindication of our Constitution against the exceptions & complaints made by Mr. Bliss Willoughby (Agent for the Separate's) to our Dissenting Brethren in England, being read and Maturely considered, this Association approved thereof & *Voted* that sᵈ Letter be forwarded to Doctʳ Avery.

Voted that the Gen'l Association shall meet in the County of Litchfield next after its session in New London County. *Voted*, that the next General Association shall meet in the County of Litchfield at the House of the Rev. Mr. Anthony Stoddard at Woodberry on the Third Tuesday of June next at 11 o'clock ante meridian; and in case he refuses, then to be at yᵉ Same time, at the House of the Rev. Mr. John Graham of the same town. Twas recommended That Every Member of the Gen'l Association for the Future come pre-pared to Preach. Test, JOSEPH FISH, Scribe.

NOTES.

1. Jonathan Merrick Pastor at North Branford from 1726 to 1769.
2. Benjamin Throop   "   at Bozrah from 1739 to 1786.
3. Elijah Sill   "   Sherman from 1751 to 1779.

1758.

[In the manuscript record book we have, between 1757 and 1759, nearly two full blank pages, and no clue to a reason why the meeting appointed for this year was not reported. In the records of Litchfield County Association, held in Salisbury May 30th of this year, the Rev. Messrs. Stoddard and Graham were appointed delegates to the meeting at Woodbury, the next June, and Mr. Graham was designated as the preacher. But no other reference to the meeting of this year is found, and like the year 1739, it is without any recorded action.]

1759.

At a Meeting of the General Association of the Colony of Connecticut, at the House of the Rev. Mr. Ebenezer White in Danbury June 19: 1759

Present

The Revd Mess^s. {
John Graham
Moses Dickinson
Jedidiah Mills
Elnathan Whitman
Daniel Humphrey
Ebenezer White
Eleazar Wheelock
John Trumble
Joseph Bellamy
Jonathan Ingersol
William Russel
}

The Rev. Mr. Moses Dickinson was chosen Moderator of the Association and the Rev. Mr. Elnathan Whitman was chosen Scribe. The Association was opened with Prayer by the Moderator. Adjourned till tomorrow Morning at 7 of the Clock.

June 20th met according to adjournment.

Resolved by this Association that as the Consociation of Churches is one great thing that the Composers of our Platform had in View, as they expressly declare that what affects all ought to be managed by all, so the Ecclesiastical Constitution of this Colony knows of no other Council whatever but a Council of the consociated Churches of the District, or in some cases a Consociation of a particular District united with a neighboring Consociation, called in, according to the Direction of the Constitution.

Resolved that it is most Expedient for the preventing the introducing of unsound and unqualified men into the Ministry, and intirely agreeable to our Ecclesiastical Constitution that the Council for the Ordination of Ministers (to whose province it belongs to examine Candidates for Ordination) should consist of the Consociation of the District to which the church belongs over which a Pastor is to be Ordained, and as this has been practiced for sundry Years by several Consociations in this Government so we recommend it to Universal Practice.

Resolved that it is most expedient that Candidates for preaching should be Examined by the Association and License given them for Preaching should be signed by the Moderator or Scribe of the Association, and accordingly we recommend it to particular Associations to come into this Practice.

An answer to a Letter from the Rev\[d] Mr. Samuel Hall of New Cheshire, voted to be sent to him.

Rev. Sir — We have received your Letter in behalf of our aggrieved Brethren at Wallingford, relative to their State, which, as you say is indeed very deplorable and in which you in their Names desire our Advice — and having considered the affair we are of the opinion that as they are at present safe under the Conduct of your Consociation, and not doubting our General Assembly will Next October take them under their Protection, and provide for their comfortable Settlement, it may be their wisest Course till then to attend on public Worship where they can, patiently submitting to present Inconvenience, in Expectation of so speedy a Relief.

Voted that the next General Association be at the Rev.^d Mr. Jonathan Merrick's in North Brantford on the 3^d Tuesday of June next.

Voted that the Rev. Mr. William Russell of Middleton preach the Concio ad Clerum in the College Hall, at the next Commencement, and in case he fail, the Rev. Mr. Lockwood of Weathersfield preach the Sermon on that Occasion.

Voted that it be recommended to the particular Associations to set forward a Subscription for the reprinting our Confession of Faith and Ecclesiastical Constitution in case the General Assembly do not Order the reprinting them at their Session in October next, and that the Rev. Mr. Williams and the Rev. Mr. Wheelock of Lebanon receive the Subscriptions and agree with the Printer for the Impression.

Unanimously passed in the Association

Test ELNATHAN WHITMAN Scribe.

NOTES.

[1]. Jedidiah Mills Pastor in Huntington from 1724 to 1773.
[2]. Daniel Humphry " Derby from 1733 to 1783.
[3]. Ebenezer White " Danbury from 1736 to 1764.
[4]. Eleazar Wheelock " Columbia from 1735 to 1770.

1760.

At a Meeting of the General Association of the Colony of Connecticut convened at the House of the Rev⁴. Jonathan Merrick in North Brandford June 17ᵗʰ : 1760

Present

The Rev⁴. Mess.
- Samuel Hall
- Jonathan Merrick
- Elnathan Whitman
- Edward Eells
- Moses Bartlit
- William Hart
- Abraham Todd [1]
- Samuel Newel
- Joseph Bellamy
- Moses Mather
- Nathan Strong [2]
- Andrew Bartholomew
- Israhiah Wetmore
- Nathanael Bartlit

The Rev⁴. Mr. Samuel Hall was chosen Moderator, and the Rev⁴ Elnathan Whitman was chosen Scribe. The Association was opened with Prayer by the Moderator.

The General Association of this Colony having in their Sessions the last year, given it as that opinion, that the Ecclesiastical Constitution of this Colony know of no Ecclesiastical Council for any Purpose whatever, but a Council of the Consociation of the District where some Ecclesiastical affair is to be transacted — This Association do further declare it as their opinion that the Council of the Consociation of New Haven County had a Right of Jurisdiction in Matters relative to Mr. Dana's Ordination, and that it was an Infringement of our Ecclesiastical Constitution for any Number of Ministers to interpose in the Affair of sᵈ

Mr Dana's Ordination in Opposition to the Consociation of s^d County. And it is further the opinion of this Association that it is the Right of our Consociated Churches to be satisfied as to the Orthodoxy and other necessary Qualifications for the ministry of any candidate for Ordination in their respective Limits before s^d Candidate is ordained.

Application having been made to this Association by a Committee of the Consociated Church in the first Society of Wallingford desiring our Advice in their present Circumstances — This Association advise s^d Consociated Church to Endeavor to obtain as many more of the Neighbouring Ministers to preach among them as they can, and as to any other Supply of Preaching we advise them to follow the Advice and Direction of the Association of New Haven County.

Voted that the next General Association be at the House of the Rev^d. Elnathan Whitman of Hartford on the third Tuesday of June Next at Eleven of the Clock in the forenoon. Passed in the General Association

Test ELNATHAN WHITMAN, Scribe.

NOTES.

[1]. Abraham Todd Pastor 2nd Greenwich 1734–1773.
[2]. Nathan Strong " North Coventry 1745–1794.

1761.

At a Meeting of the General Association of the Colony of Connecticut convened at the House of the Revd Elnathan Whitman, in Hartford June 16th 1761

Present

The Revd Mess.^s
- Jared Eliot Moderator
- Samuel Hall
- Solomon Williams
- Jonathan Merrick
- Elnathan Whitman Scribe
- William Hart
- Ebenezer Devotion
- Nathaniel Tayler [1].
- Daniel Brinsmead
- Israhiah Wetmore
- James Lockwood [2].
- Joshua Beldin [3].
- Seth Pomroy [4].
- Samuel Sherard [5].
- Robert Ross [6].

The Rev.^d Mr. Jared Eliot was chosen Moderator, and the Revd Elnathan Whitman was chosen Scribe. The Association was opened with Prayer.

Voted that an humble Address of Condolence and Congratulation, be presented to his Majesty in the Name of the Ministers of the Consociated Churches of the Colony of Connecticut in the following Words viz:

To the Kings most Excellent Majesty.

The humble Address of the Ministers of the Consociated Churches of the Colony of Connecticut convened in General Association at Hartford June 16, 1761 —

Most gracious Sovereign —

We your Majesty's most dutiful and loyal Subjects, the Ministers of the Consociated Churches of the Colony of

Connecticut in New England, most humbly beg leave to take this opportunity at our first General Convention since your Majestys accession to the Throne, to express our deep sense of the unspeakable loss your Majesty, your Kingdoms and these remote Parts of your Majesty's Dominions have sustained by the Death of his late Majesty, your royal Grandfather, and with the sincerest joy to Congratulate your Majesty's happy and peaceful Accession to the Throne of your Ancestors; the happiness of his late Majesty's wise and auspicious government so sensibly felt in every Part of his dominions, and the critical situation of the affairs of Europe, made all good men among his subjects, solicitous for the Continuance of the important Life of your royal Grandfather, and his sudden Removal would have filled his faithful subjects with much greater anxiety had not your Majesty's Succession to the Crown dispelled their fears, and opened the most pleasing Prospect of the Continuance of all the Blessings that can be Expected from the Government of the best of Kings.

Your Majesty ascends the Throne amidst the Difficulties and Uncertainties of War, we thankfully Adore the good Providence of God, which has crowned it with signal Success in every part of the World, and especially in America where the Designs of your Majesty's Enemies have been utterly defeated, important Acquisitions made to your Majesty's Territories (which we humbly hope to see united to the Crown) and the British Colonies delivered from those Distresses and Devastations to which they were frequently exposed.

Your Majesty's royal virtues, Regard to Religion and Virtue, and the true Interests of your Kingdoms, for which you are so much the Delight of your People, give us the most pleasing hopes of the greatest Security and Happiness under your Majesty's Government.

And as the Churches under our Care have always distinguished themselves by their Loyalty and Obedience, we humbly recommend them and Our Selves to your Majesty's favor and Protection, and we shall make it our constant Care to inculcate upon them Submission to your Majesty's Government and Authority, which we shall endeavour to enforce by our own example. And having our heart animated with Zeal for your Majesty's Service, we shall not cease to offer up our fervent Supplications to Almighty God, that he would multiply his Blessings upon your royal Person, that he would render your Majesty's Reign long, happy and glorious and that he would maintain the Protestant Succession in your Majestys royal House to the latest Generations.

Signed in the name and by Order of the Ministers of the Consociated Churches of the Colony of Connecticut

JARED ELIOT Moderator

Voted that the Rev.^d Mr. Jared Eliot be desired to send the foregoing Address inclosed in a Letter to the Honorable Richard Jackson Esqr, Agent of this Colony desiring him to take the earliest opportunity to present it to his Majesty, and endeavour to obtain his gracious Acceptance.

As it has been represented to this Association that the Neglect of Family Prayer is a growing Evil among our People, we recommend it to particular Associations to take the Matter into their serious Consideration and come into such Measures respecting it as shall be thought most likely to reform this growing Evil.

Voted, that the next General Association be at the house of the Rev^d Mr. Richard Salter in Mansfield on the third Tuesday of June next at Eleven of the Clock in the forenoon.

Passed in the General Association

Test ELNATHAN WHITMAN, Scribe.

NOTES.

[1]. Nathaniel Taylor Pastor in New Milford from 1748 to 1790.
[2]. James Lockwood " " Wethersfield from 1739 to 1772.
[3]. Joshua Beldin " " Newington from 1747 to 1805.
[4]. Seth Pomroy " " Greenfield from 1758 to 1769.
[5]. Samuel Sherwood " " Weston from 1757 to 1783.
[6]. Robert Ross " " 1st Bridgeport from 1753 to 1797.

1762.

At a General Association of the Colony of Connecticut at Mansfield June 15 : 1762

Present

The Rev.ᵈ Messʳˢ.
{
George Beckwith
Ebenezar Devotion
Benjamin Thoope
Hobart Eastabrook
Richard Salter¹.
Samuel Newell
Noah Welles
Samuel Lockwood².
John Ellis³.
Judah Champion⁴.
Abel Newell⁵.
Nathanael Whitaker⁶.
}

Mʳ. Beckwith was chosen Moderator and Mr. Welles Scribe. The meeting was opened with prayer by the Moderator.

The Rev. Messʳˢ. Jonathan Merrick and Warham Williams appeared in Association as delegates from the Association of New Haven County, and by order of their Constituents laid before us the Copy of a Vote of sᵈ Association, setting forth that the Rev.ᵈ Messʳˢ William Hart and John Devotion of Saybrook, and the churches of which they are Pastors had voted to hold communion with Mr. James Dana of Wallingford and those his Adherents against whom a Sentence of Non-Communion had been pronounced by a joynt Council of the Consociation of New Haven County and the South Consociation of the County of Hartford, and that the sᵈ Mr. Devotion has in his own and in the Name of the Church of which he is Pastor, declared publicly in the face of Mr. Dana's Congregation that they will hold Communion with them, and as a Testimony thereof preached to, and administered the Sacrament of Baptism amongst them — desiring the Opinion and Advice of this Association in the Affair.

Whereupon the following Case was stated for our Consideration and Resolution viz :

The Churches in a Province by explicit Agreement unite to hold a mutual Communion and Discipline, and for the more convenient carrying on the same to mutual Edification agree to divide themselves into four distinct Districts each of which have, for instance, ten Churches in them. One of the s^d Churches in one of the Districts falls into Heresy or other Scandal. The other nine Churches united in Consociation take proper Methods according to the Gospel and agreeable to s^d Union to convince and reclaim them, but they continue finally obstinate. After due waiting the s^d nine Churches pronounce a sentence of Noncommunion against the s^d offending Church. Quere — Whether their thus withdrawing Communion from s^d offending Church is to be understood as only for themselves ; or whether the other three Districts are not by virtue of their Union so included as to be obliged to carry towards the offending and censured Church as the other nine churches are obliged to do.

This Association having considered the Case declare it as their Opinion that the other three Districts, are by virtue of their Union as above s^d obliged to conduct toward the offending Church as the other nine Churches are obliged to do.

And with respect to the conduct of Messrs Hart and Devotion with their respective Churches as related above, altho' we do not look upon it as a Matter that lies before us to give a Determination in the case, yet as the Association of New Haven has desired our Opinion and Advice — Tis declared as the Opinion of this Association that they ought to be called upon by their proper Judges to assign a Reason of their Conduct and abide the Judgment that shall be given in the Case : We therefore recommend it to the Association to which they belong to Enquire into their Conduct and the Reasons of it, and according as it shall appear to take the Steps directed to in our Constitution to bring the Matter to an Issue.

Voted that the Convention of the general Association on

the third Tuesday of June next be at the House of the Rev.ᵈ Mr. Beckwith in the North Society in Lyme.

The above Voted as the doings of this Association. After which the Association concluded with Prayer by the Moderator.   Test NOAH WELLES, Scribe.

NOTES.

¹. Richard Salter   Pastor in Mansfield from 1744 to 1887.
². Samuel Lockwood   "   " Andover   "   1749 to 1791.
³. John Ellis   "   " Franklin   "   1758 to 1779.
⁴. Judah Champion   "   Litchfield   "   1758 to 1798.
⁵. Abel Newell   "   Goshen   "   1755 to 1781.
⁶. Nathaniel Whittaker " 2ⁿᵈ Norwich   "   1761 to 1769.

1763.

At a general Association of the Colony of Connecticut at Lyme 3ᵈ Parish June 21ˢᵗ 1763

Present

Rev.ᵈ Messrs. {
Grindal Rawson
Ephraim Little
George Beckwith
William Gaylord
William Hart
Ebeneza'ʳ Devotion
John Trumbal
Mark Leavenworth
Edward Dorr
Joseph Perry ¹.
}

Mr. Little was chosen Moderator and Mr. Devotion Scribe. The Meeting was opened with Prayer by the Moderator.

Voted that the Revᵈ Mr. Hart be requested for a Copy of his Sermon preached before this Association, that it may be printed if a Sufficient Sum is subscribed for the printing of it.

Voted that whereas the Western Association of the County of New London, have in Pursuance of the advice of the last general Association called Messr[s] Hart and Devotion to Account for their holding Communion with Mr. James Dana &c. and sent their Return to this Board. Altho' this Association don't look upon themselves as the proper Judges to determine the Conduct of s[d] Association or take it upon ourselves to pass any decisive Judgment in s[d] Case, Yet inasmuch as tis desired by the Delegates from s[d] Western Association that s[d] Return might be entered on the Records of this Board we do order the Scribe to Record the Same as follows —

At a Meeting of the Western Association of N. London County at the House of the Rev[d] Mr. Stephen Johnson in Lyme Oct. 6 : 1762 Present the

Rev.[d] Messr[s] Jared Eliott, Moderator, George Beckwith, William Hart, Stephen Johnson, John Devotion, Stephen Holmes, Scribe, Simeon Stoddard —

This Association having agreeable to the Advice of the General Association at the last Session, inquired into the Conduct of the Rev. Messrs William Hart and John Devotion in giving Communion to Mr. Dana and his Church and censured Members, and into the Reasons thereof: find that they have given them only that common Ministerial and Christian or Church Communion which all our consociated Churches have ever given to our neighboring Churches who are unconsociated, and that have not and do not pretend a Right to interfere in what concerns Special consociation Communion, which they fully acknowledge to be wholly in the Power of our Consociations; the matter appearing to us in this Light we do not Judge our Brethren guilty of censurable Conduct. Voted Nemine Contradicente.

A true Copy of Record —

Test STEPHEN HOLMES, Scribe.

Voted, That the next Gen. association be at The House of the Rev.[d] Mr. Benedict in Woodbury first Parish.

NOTES.

[1]. Joseph Perry Pastor in So. Windsor from 1755 to 1788.

1764.

The General Association of the Colony of Connecticut met at Woodbury the third Tuesday of June 1764.

Present

The Revd Messrs {
Jedidiah Mills
Grindal Rawson
William Seward [1].
Benjamin Strong
John Trumble
Joseph Bellamy
Ebenezer Booge [2].
Robert Ross
John Devotion [3].
Noah Benedict [4].
Benjamin Dunning [5].
}

Mr. Mills was chosen Moderator and Mr. Ross Scribe. The Meeting was opened with Prayer by the Moderator.

As the General Association is designed Especially to consult Things which tend to promote Peace and Union among the Churches in this Colony: and as it is manifest the Judgments of Consociations have in several Instances not been satisfactory, and Ministers and Churches have not looked on themselves obliged to abide by their Doings, but have acted counter to them; and as no Method has been agreed upon in which Ministers and Churches may signify their Dissatisfaction to the Consociation which they suppose have misjudged in any Case in order to get Satisfaction, and so have at one Time and another gone into Methods of testifying their Disapprobation which have given Offence: To the End therefore that some Method may be agreed upon by common Consent in which for the future particular Associations or Consociations or Ministers or Churches may inoffensively signify their Dissatisfaction and give Light to, or receive it from Consociations whose Judgment is disapproved, this Association recommends it to particular Associations to take this Matter into Consideration and to offer their Sentiments on it to the next General Association and Endeavour to point out such a Method as they look upon to be most regular.

1. In Conversation on the Point it has been queried — Whether it might not be advisable for such aggrieved Members of Churches or Associations to apply to the Association of that District, in which they suppose such Case has been misjudged with the Reasons of their Uneasiness at their Judgment, to desire them to call a Council of that Consociation to reconsider s^d Case.

2. Whether it may not be advisable upon the refusal of such Association, that the aggrieved Members of Churches, and Associations, apply to the General Association with their Reasons as aforesaid desiring them if they think the Case requires it, to recommend it to s$^{d.}$ Association to call a Council of s^d District to reconsider the Matter.

The following questions were bro't to the Association which were thus answered viz.

1. Has a Husband any Right to exercise Authority over his Wife in Cases wherein there are different Sentiments respecting Religion? Ans. No.

2. Whether for the Husband to reflect upon, or treat his wife with any Bitterness or Unkindness on Account of different Sentiments and Practice as abovesaid is wicked and abusive? Ans. Yes.

3. Whether it be lawful and right for the Wife out of Compliance with her Husband to conform to his Practice contrary to her Sentiments where there are religious Differences? Ans. No.

The next General Association was appointed to be at the House of the Rev.^{d} Mr. Dickinson in Norwalk on the third Tuesday in June next. The Association Voted the above and foregoing as their Doings

Test ROBERT ROSS, Scribe.

Notes.

[1]. William Seward Pastor in Killingworth from 1738 to 1782.
[2]. Ebenezer Booge " West Avon from 1751 to 1767.
[3]. John Devotion " Westbrook from 1757 to 1802.
[4]. Noah Benedict " 1st Woodbury from 1760 to 1811.
[5]. Benjamin Dunning " Marlboro from 1762 to 1773.

1765.

At a Convention of the general Association of the Colony of Connecticut at Norwalk in the County of Fairfield on the 3d Tuesday of June AD 1765

Present

The Revd Messieurs
- Moses Dickinson
- George Beckwith
- Edward Eelles Moderator
- Daniel Humphrey
- Mark Lavenworth
- Noah Welles
- Edward Dorr
- Nathaniel Taylor
- Israhiah Wetmore
- Nathaniel Bartlett
- Hezekiah Gold
- Stephen Holmes [1].
- Nathaniel Hooker [2].
- Enoch Huntington [3].
- Joseph Huntington [4].

The Rev^d Mr. Eells was chosen Moderator and Mr. Wetmore, Scribe. The Meeting was opened with Prayer offered by the Moderator. Discoursed of sundry Matters relative to State of the Churches and the Interest of Religion. Adjourned till 7 o'Clock tomorrow Morning.

Met according to adjournment.

Whereas it was recommended by the last general Association to the several particular Associations in this Colony to prepare and send into the next general Association some expedient that might be made use of in order for aggrieved Persons to obtain a rehearing of those Cases wherein they conceive the Consociation have misjudged and inasmuch as the particular Associations have not in general thought fit to send in to this Board any Proposals for the above mentioned Purposes, this Association is of the Opinion that the Rule of the Platform is so plain in all such cases and so well understood and practiced upon by the Churches in general that no further Provision is needful to be made.

The following questions were proposed to this Association for their Consideration and Resolution — viz Ques^n

1st. Whether ye present difficult State of the C^{hhes} of this Colony respecting the Support and Continuance of a learned orthodox Ministry doth require any further Provision to be made therefor?

Resolved in the Affirmative.

Q^n II Whether it be prudent & advisable for this Association to go into any Measures to procure any further Provision for the Purpose afores^d?

Resolved in the Affirmative.

Whereupon this Association do unanimously recommend it to the Several particular Associations of this Colony to take the Matter into their Serious Consideration & appoint some sutable Persons to meet at Hartford in May next at the Election to advise with each Other and prosecute such Methods as upon the whole may be thought most effectual to Remedy the Evil complained of: and in the mean time do recommend it to the Members of this Association to take all Sutable Opportunity of advising with any of the principal Gentlemen in the Government what may be the most proper Measures to be pursued in this Case.

A Motion was made to this Association concerning the Decency & Propriety of making the public reading of the

Sacred Scriptures a Part of the publick Worship in our C^hhs; and as Uniformity in said Practice is greatly to be desired this Association do earnestly recommend it to the several particular Associations to promote said Practice among the several C^hhs.

The next general Association is appointed to be at the House of the Rev^d Mr. Ruggles in Guilford at 11 o'Clock ante Meridian. The above & foregoing Voted as the Doings of this Association.

Teste ISRAHIAH WETMORE, Scribe.

NOTES.

1. Stephen Holmes   Pastor Centerbrook   1757 to 1773.
2. Nathaniel Hooker   "   West Hartford 1757 to 1870.
3. Enoch Huntington   "   1st Middletown 1762 to 1809.
4. Joseph Huntington   "   South Coventry 1763 to 1794.

1766.

At a General Association of the Ministers in the Colony of Connecticut at Guilford the 3^d Tuesday in June 1766 at the House of the Rev^d Mr. Thomas Ruggles,

Present

Thomas Ruggles
George Beckwith
Edward Eells
Joseph Bellamy
Moses Mather
Joseph Fowler
Samuel Sherwood
Nath^ll Bartlit
Judah Champion
Elizer Goodrich
Noah Wetmore
Levi Hart

The Rev⁴. Thoˢ Ruggles was chosen Modʳ, Edward Eells Scribe.

The meeting was opened with prayer by the Moderator.

There was a motion made to this association by the Synod of New York and Philadelphia contained in minutes from the Synod Book & a Letter, which are as follows.

A minute from the Synod Book of New York and Philadelphia of May 29 P. M. anno Salutis 1766 viz:

An Overture was made by some members that we ought to endeavour to obtain some Correspondence betwen this Synod & the Consociated Churches of our Brethen in Connecticut a Draught of a letter from this Synod to them was brought in, read, & approved — The Revᵈ Mr. Elihu Spencer moderator, the Rev. Mr. John Ewing & Mr. Patrick Alison are Desired to present this Letter & Confer with our Brethren upon this affair, and provided it shall seem meet to our Rev.ᵈ Brethren to attend to this our proposal so far as to appoint Commissioners from their body to meet with Commissioners from ours, we appoint the Rev. Dʳ Francis Alison, the Revᵈ Messʳ John Roger, Timothy Jones, William Tennent Senʳ, Elisha Kent, John Smith, John Blair, & Samuel Buel to meet with them at such time & place as the Rev.ᵈ Brethren from Connecticut shall agree. The Rev.ᵈ Mr. John Rogers is appointed to give the Committee notice of what the associated Brethren will do Relative to this matter.

A true Copy

MATTHEW WILSON Synod Clerk.

Rev.ᵈ & Dʳ Brethren — The Synod of New York & Philadelphia at their annual meeting in May 1766 have among many other expedients to promote the interests of the Redeemer's Kingdom, concluded upon the most mature Deliberation, that a general meeting of Delegates both from your Chhˢ & our Presbyteries would answer this important purpose — our earnest Desire to accomplish so good an end has engaged us to embrace this opportunity of your next general association to propose the matter to your Serious Deliberation & to invite you to a general Consultation about such things as may have a hopeful tendency to promote & defend the Common Cause of Religion against the attacks of its various Enemies. As we are all Brethren, embarked in the same Interest, perfectly agreed in Doctrine & worship, Substantially pursuing the same method of Discipline & C^{hh} Government, & we trust all animated with the Same Laudable Zeal to advance the Kingdom of our Common Lord, we cannot but hope for your ready concurrence with our invitation. Your Good Sense & general acquaintance with human nature must necessarily lead you to see that a more intimate acquaintance with each other's views & Designs will unable us with greater Harmony & Consistence & of consequence of greater Success, to support the Common Cause in which we are all equally engaged. A general agreement in any measures that may be adopted to preserve our Religious liberties against all Encroachments, and to Bless the benighted Heathen on our Borders with the glorious light of the Gospel must promise desirable Success.

From the best information we can obtain about the Constitution of your C^{hhs} we are persuaded that our proposal is not impracticable, & it will give us a sensible pleasure to find that your Extensive charity & readiness to promote the Kingdom of Christ have induced you to concert such measures as will be best adapted to accomplish so important an end.

We have appointed the Rev^d Mr. Elihu Spencer Mr. John Ewing & Mr. Patrick Alison to wait upon you at your next General Association to Deliver you our Letter & to converse with you at large on the Subject of this proposal.

Signed by order of Synod by

ELIHU SPENCER, Mod^r.

The Association's Reply is as follows — Whereas a proposal has been made to this General Association by the Revd Synod of New York & Philadelphia, Representing, that they are Strictly United with us in Doctrine & worship as contained in the Westminster Confession of faith & Catechisms, & that the great & general interest of the Redeemer's Kingdom would be happily promoted, the common cause of Religion & virtue Strengthened & Defended, whilst mutual benevolence & Brotherly love would be cultivated by a General union, agreement & Correspondence with us, so far & in such manner as is consistent & in no Degree interfering with their & our Respective internal State & order of government & Discipline; and that it will give them great Satisfaction to meet a number of our Ministers at a Suitable time & place to converse with them upon a plan & articles of such desired Union —

We therefore, having maturely considered their proposal are unanimously agreed to use our influence to promote a compliance with it thro' this Colony, and we do in order thereto advise the Several Associations to appoint one or more of their body to meet Commissioners from the Synod beforementioned at New York the first Wednesday in November next to converse with them upon a plan & articles of such desired Union; to be laid before the Several associations for their Concurrence, & to be prepared for the consideration of the next general association, & then to be completed.

Voted in the Affirmative.

A copy of a Letter wrote to Mr. Rodger of New York —

Guilford June 17 : 1766

Rev.^{d} & Dear S^r

With gratitude we have Received the friendly proposal from your Revd Synod, relative to a General Union, and our ready Compliance with it comes enclosed, and we shall Rejoice if the Design may be happily carried into Execution, & answer the good & valuable Ends in view. And may the Glorious & Blessed time approach, when love & union may prevail among all Denominations of Christians thr'o the world. We are Revd Sir

Your affectionate Brethren
Signed by order of the Association
THOMAS RUGGLES Mod^r.

Voted, upon a motion to this Association respecting the Charge given in the Ordination of a Minister to his office & work, as it is by the authority of all the Elders present & acting in the affair, as well as with the joynt Consent of the whole Council, it is recommended to the particular associations that in this Business of ordination whoever is appointed to give the Charge to the person to be ordained should first lay before the Council the form he intends to use for their concurrence & approbation, and that the Charge be given in the first person Plural.

Voted that the next General Association in June be at the Rev.^d Mr. Enoch Huntington's in Middletown.

Voted that this association be adjourned to the first day of July next to meet at the Chapel Hall in New Haven, and then an address should be prepared to be presented to his Majesty King George the 3^d on account of the Royal favor in repealing the Act that was so grievous to the Northern Colonies.

Recorded by EDWARD EELLS Scribe

July 1st 1766 — This Association met at the Chapel Hall in New Haven according to adjournment and adjourned untill tomorrow at 11^{oc} in the forenoon and continued by adjournment until the 3^d day, then adjourned to the 9th of Sept. next to meet at the Chapel Hall in New Haven

Sept. 11 This Association meet according to adjournment, and upon the unanimous motion & Desire of the large Convention of Ministers present on occasion of the Commencement the Moderator of this association is requested by writing to Desire the Rev. Mr. Roger that the intended interview of Deligates from the Rev. Synod of New York &c and the several associations of this Colony may be at Jamaica on Long Island and not at New York as was at first proposed, where it could not be attended without danger of the Small Pox

at this Meeting the Rev. W^m. Russell Joyn'd this association } Voted in the affirmative

Recorded by EDWARD EELLS, Scribe.

NOTES.

1. Elizer Goodrich Pastor at Durham from 1756–1797.
2. Noah Wetmore   "   Bethel from 1760–1784.
3. Levi Hart   "   Griswold " 1762–1808.

1767.

At a meeting of the General Association of the Colony of Connecticut at the House of the Rev⁴ Enoch Huntington in Middletown June 16 : 1767

Present —

The Rev.⁴ Messʳˢ
- Thomas Ruggles
- George Beckwith
- William Hart
- James Lockwood
- Edward Dorr
- William Russell
- Warham Williams¹.
- Samuel Sherwood
- David Ripley².
- Elijah Sill
- Joel Bordwell³.
- Enoch Huntington
- Noadiah Warner⁴.
- Joseph Huntington

The Revⁿᵈ Thomas Ruggles was chosen Moderator and William Russell, Scribe.

The Association was opened with Prayer.

This Association being informed by the Delegates that the several particular Associations in the Colony have considered & approved the Design of a Convention at New Haven next September, agreeable to the motion made at the Convention in Elizabeth-Town last November, and have appointed Delegates to attend it; desire the Moderator to signify the same to the Revd Synod by a Letter to the Revnd John Rogers of New York. Which is as follows— Revnd S^r

By order of the General Association now regularly convened at Middletown I am desired to inform you, and by you the Revnd Synod of New York & Philadelphia, That the proposed Convention at New Haven in Sept^{br} next has been considered and approved by the particular Associations thro the Government, and they have appointed Delegates to attend the Convention agreed to by the Revnd Convention at Elizabeth-Town in November last. And to assure you that with great Respect we are your Brethren in the Faith & Fellowship of our common Lord Jesus Christ.

Voted that the following Questions be recommended to the Consideration of the several Associations in the Colony and that they be desired to transmit their Sentiments to the next General Association.

1st. Whether Lay-Ordination is valid?

2. Whether Baptism administered by Persons who have only Lay-Ordination is valid?

Item. That the General Association on the third Tuesday in June next, be at the House of the Revd Joseph Huntington in Coventry.

Unanimously passed in the Association.

Test W^M RUSSELL Scribe.

NOTES.

[1]. Warham Williams Pastor in Northford from 1750–1788.
[2]. David Ripley   "   Abington   "   1753–1778.
[3]. Joel Bordwell   "   Kent   "   1758–1811.
[4]. Noadiah Warner   "   1st Danbury "   1765–1768.

1768.

At a general association of the pastors of the consociated churches in the colony of Connecticut convened by delegation at Coventry June 21 : 1768 — present

    Solomon Williams
    George Beckwith
    John Trumble
    Noah Welles
    Jonathan Lee [1].
    Eliphalet Williams [2].
    Elijah Mason [3].
    Samuel Lockwood
    Elijah Lathrop [4].
    Judah Champion
    D[r] Nathaniel Whitaker
    Benjamin Trumble [5].
    Joseph Huntington
    Hezekiah Ripley [6].

Mr. Williams was chosen Moderator and Mr. Welles Scribe. The Association opened with prayer by the moderator.

Voted that the thanks of this body be returned to the Rev.[d] D[r] Chauncy of Boston for the good service he has done to the cause of religion, liberty and truth in his judicious answer to the appeal for an american episcopate, and in his defence of the Newengland churches and colonies against the unjust reflections cast upon them in the bishop of Landaff's sermon before the society for propagating the gospel in foreign parts : and that the moderator present the same to the Doc.[r]; and cause this resolve to be published in one of the Boston Newspapers.

Voted that the thanks of this body be returned to William Livingston Esq[r]. attorney at law in New York, for his late vindication of the Newengland churches and planters against the injurious reflections and unjust aspersions cast upon them in the bishop of Landaff's late sermon before the society for propagating the gospel, contained in his manly and Spirited Letter to his Lordship: and that the scribe be desired to transmit this resolve to Mr Livingston and cause it to be published in one of the New York Newspapers.

Voted that Mr Dickinson who is appointed a delegate to the general convention at Elizabeth town in october next, be desired to preach at the opening of the convention, and in case of his failing, Mr Williams another of our delegates is desired to attend that Service.

Adjourned to 7 °Clock tomorrow morning. Met according to adjournment.

Voted that the general association in June next be at the house of the Rev.^{d} M^r. Lord at Norwich, and in case any circumstances should render it inexpedient to meet there, then that the Revd Mr Harts of Preston be the place of meeting.

The association finding some inconveniences attending the present practice of this body in delaying the public lecture upon these occasions to the second day of the session, ordered that it be declared as our advice, that for the future the lecture be attended on the first day of the session.

Whereas some dispute arose in the last general convention concerning the admission of members to vote in s^d convention; and whereas we understand that the Rev^d the Synod of New York and Philadelphia, in order to put an end to that dispute for time to come did at their last meeting agree that though any gentleman who shall think proper may be freely permitted to be present in convention, yet none but the delegates shall be allowed a vote, this association heartily concur with the above limitation; and moreover give it as our opinion and advice that none but the delegates shall be admitted publicly to debate any case before the convention unless particularly requested by the body so to do. And it is further declared as the opinion and advice of this body, that it is not expedient for the future that any of our associations delegate more than two of their members to the general convention. Finally we think it may be advisable that in any future general convention nothing be deemed as an act of the convention, considered as the voice of the united body but what has the major vote of the respective members that shall be present both from the Synod and from the consociated pastors in Connecticut.

Whereas the Rev^d D^r. Whitaker lately returned from Great Britain hath represented to this Body the Kind & Charitable Disposition of the good & Pious People there manifested in the generous & charitable contributions to the Support of Dr. Wheelock's Indian Academy for the Promotion of Christianity and Civility among the Savage Indians on this Continent; We are greatly Pleased to find that the Hearts of our Dear Brethren on the other Side the Atlantic are so united with our's in the truly Evangelical and noble Design which the Hearts of the Pious in this Country have been & still are so intent upon; and do by this testify our grateful Sense of their goodness & liberality and express our cordial Desires That the Best of Blessings may rest on all the Pious Benefactors, & that Heaven would still prosper the important Design. And 'Tis Desired that Dr Wheelock & Dr Whitaker would Transmit this to their Friends in Great Britain to be communicated in such manner as they think proper as a public Testimony of our gratitude.

The above Voted as the Doings of this association. concluded with prayer.

       Test NOAH WELLES Scribe.

NOTES.

[1]. Jonathan Lee Pastor at Salisbury from 1744 to 1788.
[2]. Eliphalet Williams " " East Hartford from 1748 to 1801.
[3]. Elijah Mason Pastor at Chester from 1767 to 1770.
[4]. Elijah Lothrop " " Gilead " 1752 to 1797.
[5]. Benjamin Trumble " " North Haven from 1760 to 1820.
[6]. Hezekiah Ripley " " Greens Farms " 1767 to 1821.

1769.

At a meeting of the Delegates from the several Associations of the Colony of Connecticut at the House of the Rev[d] M[r]. Lord of Norwich June 20th 1769

  present —
    Solomon Williams
    Grindal Rawson
    Nathan[11] Eells
    Ephraim Little
    Joseph Fish
    George Beckwith
    Ebenez[r] Devotion
    Benjamin Throop
    Moses Mather
    Warham Williams
    John Willard [1].
    Cotton Mather Smith [2].
    William Patten [3].
    Simon Waterman [4].
    Isaac Lewis [5].

M[r] Solomon Williams was chosen Moderator and M[r] Devotion Scribe. The Association opened with Prayer by the Moderator.

The following unanimously voted viz:

At a Session of the General Association of the Ministers of the Colony of Connecticut, at Norwich June 20 1769.

This Association taking into serious Consideration the dark and threatening Aspect of divine Providence upon our Nation and Land in regard to their civil Liberties and public Interest: as also the great decay of practical Godliness and the Prevalence of Iniquity, think it desirable that a Day be set apart for public Fasting and Prayer, to humble ourselves, under the righteous Hand of God, and supplicate the Throne of his Grace for the removal of the Calamities we are under and to prevent those which seem to be impending. And above all that he would pour out his Spirit upon the Churches and people of the Land, revive decaying Religion and enlarge the Kingdom of the Redeemer. And accordingly agree for ourselves, and recommend it to the Brethren in the Ministry, to our own Churches and the Churches throughout the Colony to set apart the last thursday of August next for the Purpose aforesaid, earnestly desiring both Ministers and people, unanimously to join in the Seasonable, solemn and important Duty. And those of our Brethren and their Churches, that cannot conveniently attend it upon the Day aforesaid, to them we recommend it that they attend it on some other Day.

Voted that the next general Association be at the House of the Revd Mr Taylor in N. Milford.

Test EBENEZ^R DEVOTION Scribe

NOTES.

[1]. John Willard Pastor in Stafford from 1757 to 1807.
[2]. John Cotton Smith Pastor in Sharon from 1755 to 1804.
[3]. William Patten Pastor 2nd Hartford from 1767 to 1773.
[4]. Simon Waterman Pastor 2nd Wallingford from 1761 to 1787.
[5]. Isaac Lewis Pastor in Wilton from 1768 to 1786.

1770.

The General Association met according to Appointment at the House of the Revᵈ Mʳ. Taylor in New Milford on the third Tuesday of June 1770.

Present the Revd Messieurs
>Daniel Humphrey
>Robert Silliman ¹.
>Jonathan Lee
>Joshua Belding
>Nathaniel Taylor
>Samuel Sherwood
>Joseph Strong ².
>Nathaniel Bartlet
>Robert Ross
>Benajah Roots ³.
>John Smalcy ⁴.
>Eliphalet Huntington ⁵.
>David Brunson ⁶.

Mʳ. Humphrey was chosen Moderator and Mʳ Ross Scribe — The Association was opened with Prayer by the Moderator. The Association Adjourned till 7 o'clock tomorrow morning — Met According to Adjournment — Mʳ Lee prayed at the Desire of the Moderator — the General Association observe with much Grief and Concern that various Scandals prevail among Sundry of the members of our Churches, and that some absent themselves frequently from public Worship and the holy Communion — and the great Neglect of Gospel Discipline, and therefore earnestly recommend it to the Several Associations to take this Important Matter into their Immediate and Serious Consideration and prosecute such measures as they shall think most expedient to revive brotherly Watchfulness & Church Discipline.

The Revᵈ Mʳ Lockwood of Wethersfield appointed to preach the Sermon at the publick Convention at Elizabeth Town, and in case of his failure M[r] Ross — the next General Association is appointed to be at the House of the Rev[d] M[r] Bartlet in Reading on the third Tuesday in June next 1771. The public Lecture was preached by M[r] Lee after which the Association was dismissed.

Test ROBERT ROSS, Scribe.

NOTES.

[1]. Robert Silliman   Pastor at New Canaan 1742–1771.
[2]. Joseph Strong   "   Granby 1752–1779.
[3]. Benajah Roots   "   Simsbury 1757–1772.
[4]. John Smaley   "   New Britain 1758–1810.
[5]. Eliphalet Huntington   "   Clinton 1764–1777.
[6]. David Brunson   "   Oxford 1764–1806.

1771.

The General Association of the Colony of Connecticut convened according to Appointment at the House of the Rev.[d] Nath[nl] Bartlet in Reading on the 3[d] Tuesday of June 1771.

Present the Rev[d] Mess[rs]

Joseph Bellamy
Jonathan Ingersol
Nathan Strong
Nath[l] Taylor
Joseph Strong
Nathan[l] Bartlett
Robert Ross
Simon Waterman
Stephen Hawley [1].
Benj[n] Duning [2].

Dr. Bellamy was chosen Moderator and Mr. Waterman scribe. The Association was opened with prayer by the Moderator. The Rev. John Norton is also now present.

Whereas the General Association did at their last sessions recommend to the several particular Associations to take into their serious Consideration the Important Matter of Church Discipline, and prosecute such methods as they shall think most expedient to promote Brotherly Watchfulness and best answer the ends of Church Discipline — and this Association finding that no Return from any Association hath been made to this Body relative hereto; and being desirous of Promoting so good a Design, and observing with grief and concern the declining State of our Churches for Want of Gospel Discipline — Do *recommend* to the several Associations to take this matter into their serious consideration; *and Desire* they would send to the next General Association their Resolutions or Opinion on the following Questions viz:

1st. Whether it is not the indispensible Duty of Christian Churches to maintain Gospel Discipline? 2ly What can be done to restore gospel Discipline in our Churches?

The Revd Messrs Taylor and Ross according to the appointment of the last General Convention laid before the Body the importance of punctually attending every General Convention, particularly the Next at Norwalk — and 'tis hereby earnestly recommended to the Delegates now chosen that they do attend. The next General Association is appointed to be at the House of the Revd Mr John Trumble in Westbury on the 3d Tuesday of June 1772.

Test SIMON WATERMAN Scribe.

NOTES.

[1]. Stephen Hawley Pastor in Bethany   from 1763 to 1804.
[2]. Benjamin Duning   "   Marlborough "   1762 to 1773.

1772.

At a general Association of y⁰ Pastors of y⁰ Consociated Churches in y⁰ Colony of Connecticut convened by Deligation at Westbury, June 16: 1772 present the Rev⁴ Mess⁻ˢ

> Elnathan Whitman
> John Trumbull
> Moses Marther
> Samuel Newell
> Benjⁿ Woodbridge
> Jonathan Lee
> Samuel Lockwood
> Daniel Brimsmaid '.
> Elijah Sill
> Elijah Lathrop
> John Devotion

Mr. Whitman was chosen Moderator & Mʳ. Lockwood Scribe. The Association was opened with a Sermon by Mʳ. Woodbridge.

Voted, that whereas the last general Association recommended to the several particular Associations Two Questions respecting a reviving of Discipline in our Churches for their opinions, & but Three of them have returned their answers, the other are desired to Send in their answer to yᵉ next general Association, and yᵉ Deligates from those Six are desired to Inform their respective Associations of this Resolve.

Voted Instructions to the Deligates of the Several Associations appointed to attend the next general Convention to meet at Elizabeth Town, the last Wednesday but one in Sepʳ 1772 — Revᵈ Brethren, Whereas some of the Clergy of the Church of England have showed great Asseduity in Soliciting an American Episcopate, and Petitions (as we are informed) have been perfered to his Majesty the archbishop of Canterbury &c by Mess.ʳˢ Cooper & Horox requesting yᵉ same — we Inform you that 'tis the advice of this Association that you heartily concur with the Southern Gentlemen in counteracting any Motions that have or shall be made for s^d Episcopate in such manner as shall be most Convenient in said Convention.

Voted That the Revd Sa^ll Clark who is appointed Deligate to the next general Convention at Elizabethtown be desired to open s^d Convention with a Sermon, & in case of his failing Mr Cotton M. Smith another of our Deligates is Desired to perform that service.

In reference to a number of Questions Sent to this Board from ye Revd Nathl Sherman of Mount Carmel for their Resolution.

Voted 1st That a Minister whose Usefulness is beyond all doubt at an end with his People ought to be willing to resign and may be Warrantably Dismissed without his consent although guilty of neither Herise nor Scandal & yet great care ought to be taken that Ministers are not Injured in their Temporal Interests.

Voted 2^ly If any Minister thinks himself Injured in Temporalities by a too Sudden Dismission thro' the unreasonable Clamour of his People, & the People refuse to come into any reasonable Method to do him Justice as to his Temporal Interest, he can have no Redress unless at ye Civil Board.

3^ly If any injury is done to any Minister's Character in the Result of the Consociation that Dismisses him, ye only Method for Redress in ye Case is to Desire a Rehearing at ye Same Board.

4^ly No Cause can be removed from a Consociation after Judgment is given to another Board to be reheard and redetermined, Unless by agreement of ye Parties concerned, and Concurrence of the Consociation.

Voted, To desire the Rev^d. Noah Wells, Standing Register of ye general Convention annually to lay before this Board the Doings of s^d Convention.

Voted That the next general Association be at the House of the Revd Sa^ll Newell in New Cambridge. The above

Voted as the Doings of this Association. Concluded with Prayer.

Test Sa[ll] Lockwood, Scribe.

Notes.

[1]. Daniel Brinsmaid Pastor in Washington from 1749 to 1785.

1773.

At a Meeting of the general Association of the Colony of Connecticut at the House of the Rev.[d] Sam[ll] Newell in *New Cambridge June 15th 1773 —

Present

The Rev.[d] Mess.[rs]
{
George Beckwith
Hez[h] Bissel
W[m] Seward
Jonathan Ingersol
Sam[ll] Newell
Nathan Strong
Elijah Sill
Daniel Welch [1].
Robert Ross
Benj[n] Boardman [2].
Ammi R. Robbins [3].
Andrew Stores [4].
W[m] Drummond [5]
Cyprian Strong [6].
Sam[ll] J[o]. Mills [7].
John Foot [8]
}

The Rev.[d] George Beckwith was chosen Moderator — Benj[n] Boardman Scribe. The Council was opened with Prayer offered by the Moderator. The Rev[d] Hez[h] Bissel preached a Sermon. Adjourned till 7 oclock to Morrow Morning.

June 16th 7 o'Clock A. M. Convened according to adjournment, entered upon Business and Papers were read on the

Subject of Chh Discipline, sent in from several of the particular associations viz: one from the Eastern District of Fairfield County : — Do. from the South District of Hartford County — Do. from Windham County — this remark toward y̧ᵉ close. Do. from New London County — Do. from Litchfield County — Do. from New Haven County — Do. from Hartford North District — and after having taken into consideration yᵉ above said Papers touching Chh Discipline,

Voted That the Revᵈ Messieurs Edward Eells, Elizur Goodrich, Benjⁿ Boardman, Enoch Huntington and Cyprian Strong be a Comᵗᵉᵉ to collect some general Things into form from said Papers or Exhibits and prepare the same to be laid in before the next Genˡ Association for their further Consideration.

Voted also that the next General Association be at the House of the Revᵈ Solomon Williams at Lebanon in Windham County on the third Tuesday of June next — and in case anything should intervene rendering it inconvenient to Meet at the sᵈ Mr. William's then to meet at the House of the Rev.ᵈ Daniel Welch of Mansfield at the afforesaid Time & in said County.

The above voted as the Doings of this Association & then concluded with Prayer.

Attested p'r Benjⁿ Boardman, Scribe

Notes.   *Now Bristol.

1. Daniel Welch Pastor in North Mansfield — 1752 to 1782.
2. Benjamin Boardman Pastor in Middle Haddam — 1762 to 1783.
3. Ammi R. Robbins Pastor in Norfolk — 1761 to 1813.
4. Andrew Stores   "   Plymouth — 1765 to 1785.
5. William Drummond "   New Canaan — 1772 to 1777.
6. Cyprian Strong   "   1ˢᵗ Portland — 1767 to 1811.
7. Samuel J. Mills   "   Torringford — 1769 to 1822.
8. John Foot   "   Cheshire — 1767 to 1813.

1774.

At a General Association of the Pastors of the Consociated churches in the Colony of Connecticut convened by Delegates at the House of the Rev^d. Daniel Welch in Mansfield June 21st 1774 —

Present —

Rev^d. Messrs. Benjamin Throop
James Cogswell
Stephen Johnson [1].
Warham Williams
Samuel Lockwood
Elijah Lathrop
Daniel Welch
John Ellis
Simon Waterman
William Drummond
John Bliss
Theodore Hinsdale [2].
Hezekiah Ripley
Ebenezer Baldwin [3].

The Rev^d Mr. Throop was chosen Moderator & M^r. Baldwin, Scribe.

The Meeting was opened with prayer by the Moderator. The association then proceeded to business. The Report of a Committee appointed at the last association to draw up something upon Church Discipline proper to be recommended by this association was read. Likewise some Tho'ts upon the Subject of Discipline were exhibited from the western association of Fairfield County.

The Rev^d. Messrs Waterman, Drummond, & Baldwin were appointed a Committee to draw a Draft of a Letter of Condolence to the Ministers of Boston under the present melancholy circumstances of that Town.

The Rev^d. Messrs Cogswell, Johnson & Lockwood were appointed a Committee to draw up something upon the Subject of Church Discipline proper to be recommended to the Several Churches of this Colony.

The Rev.[d] Samuel Lockwood is appointed to preach the Sermon at the opening of the next Convention at Elizabeth Town, & in case of his Failure the Rev[d] Mr. Baldwin is appointed.

Adjourned till tomorrow morning 7 oclock, June 22. Met according to adjournment.

This association taking into Consideration the State of y[e] Settlements now forming in the Wilderness to the Westward & North-westward of us, who are mostly destitute of a preached Gospel, many of which are of our Brethren Emigrants from this Colony, think it advisable that an attempt should be made to send missionaries among them, and for obtaining a Support for such Missionaries would recommend it to the several Ministers in this Colony to promote a Subscription among their people for this purpose. Upon which it was Voted that the preceding conclusion together with the form of a Subscription be printed & sent to the several Ministers in this Colony. a Lecture was then attended, the Rev[d] M[r] Cogswell preached from Phil. 2: 1, 2 —

The doings of the last General Convention were read before this association & were well accepted. The Rev.[d] Mess[rs] Cogswell & Johnson were appointed to compleat the Draft of a Letter to the Ministers of Boston.

The Committee appointed to draw up a Draft upon Church Discipline made their Report which was ordered to lye on File.

The Rev.[d] Mess[rs] Noah Wells, Sam[el] Lockwood & Elijah Lathrop were appointed a Committee to draw up a Draft upon Church Government to be presented to this Body at their adjourned sessions in Sept[r] next. The Committee appointed prepared a Draft of a Letter to the Ministers of Boston which after Correction was accepted & is as follows —

Rev.[d] & dear Sirs, We your brethren of the Colony of Connecticut met by Delegation from the several Counties in general association, at our annual meeting, cannot but feel deeply impressed with the present melancholy threatened Situation of America in general & the distressed state of the Town of Boston in particular suffering the Severe resentment of the British Parliament by which the Subsistence of Thousands is taken away. We readily embrace this opportunity, to manifest our hearty Sympathy with you in your present Distresses. We consider you as suffering in the common cause of America; in the cause of civil Liberty, which, if taken away, we fear would involve the ruin of Religious Liberty also. Gladly would we contribute everything in our Power for your encouragement and Relief; however our Situation enables us to do little more than to express our sincere, affectionate Concern, & with fervent addresses to commend your Cause, & the Cause of America — the Cause of Liberty & above all of Religion to the Father of Mercies, who can easily afford effectual Relief; who hath the Hearts of all at his Disposal & can turn them as he pleases. We feel deeply sensible what a heavy Load must lie upon the minds of the Ministers of Boston — enough to sink their Spirits unless armed with vigor, Christian Fortitude & Resolution. In hopes it may afford you some Consolation we assure you of our sincere Condolence and unremitted prayers in your Behalf; and that we shall in every way suitable to our Character and Station use our Influence with the good People of this Colony to concur in every proper measure calculated to afford Relief to America in general, & the distressed Town of Boston in Particular. We pray that the Ministers of Boston may be inspired by the great Head of the Church with Wisdom sufficient for their Direction in such a critical Day as the present. And we cannot but hope the united Prayers of America may obtain that audience in Heaven which will ensure Salvation to us; and That God would give them & their People Firmness, Unanimity, Patience, Prudence & every Virtue which they need to support them under their heavy trials, & enable them to stand firm in the glorious Cause of Liberty; express such a Temper & exhibit such an Example as shall be well pleasing to God, & recommend them to the Compassion & Favor of their fellow men. We earnestly pray that God would humble us all under a deep sense of our numerous Transgressions & Criminal Declensions; show us the absolute necessity of Repentance & Reformation, humble us under his mighty hand & pour out a Spirit of Fervent Supplication on you, on us, & all his people in this Land."

Voted that there be a standing Register appointed to keep the Records of this association & the Revd Mr Trumbull of North Haven is appointed the present Register. The next general association in June 1775 is appointed to be at the house of the Revd Mr Throop at New Concord in Norwich.

The Southern association of Hartford County having neglected to appoint one to preach the *Conscio ad Clerum*, the day following the next Commencement, this association do therefore appoint the Revd Edward Eells of Middletown to preach the Sermon at that Time. This association is adjourned to the day after the next Commencement to meet at Newhaven in the College Chapel at 8 o'Clock in the Morning. The session was concluded with prayer by the Moderator.

Test EBENEZER BALDWIN, Scribe.

NOTES.

[1]. Stephen Johnson   Pastor at Old Lyme from 1746 to 1786.
[2]. Theodore Hinsdale   "   North Windsor 1766 to 1795.
[3]. Ebenezer Baldwin   "   1st Danbury   1770 to 1776.

1774 Continued.

The general association of the Pastors of the Consociated Churches of the Colony of Connecticut convened by Delegation at Newhaven Sept. 15th 1774 according to adjournment—

Present

Rev.d Messrs Benjamin Throop
Thomas Canfield '.
Samuel Lockwood
Elijah Lathrop
Nathaniel Bartlett
John Ellis
Simon Waterman
John Bliss
Theodore Hinsdale
Hezekiah Ripley
Ebenezar Baldwin
Jehu Miner ².

The Revd Mr Wells read before this Body a Draught for the Improvement of Discipline in our Churches, according to appointment from this Body.

The association then entered upon further Consideration of the Subject of sending Missionaries to the Scattered Settlements in the Wilderness to the Northwestward, and came into the following Conclusions.

1st The General Association find so much encouragement relative to the Support of Missionaries to be sent into the back Settlements, that they think it advisable to appoint 2 Missionaries to go upon this business next Spring.

2. That one person be appointed in each County to receive the Subscriptions or Donations made, or that shall be hereafter made for this purpose in sd County. They to give their Receipt to the Persons from whom they Receive them.

3. That a Committee of three Persons be appointed to receive these Donations from the Receivers in the several Coun-

ties & to give their Receipts therefor — This Committee to appoint to the Missionaries their Support — to pay such sums to them, as they may see proper to appoint from the Donations received by them. They to direct the Missionaries in any thing they shall Judge Necessary where not particularly directed by the general association. They also may appoint other Missionaries in case of the failure of any appointed by this Body. They to account to the General Association yearly, for the Disposal of the Monies rec^d by them — to lay before this Body the proceedings of the Missionaries — their success — the State of the Place wherein they may discharge their Missions &c. This Committee to continue during the Pleasure of the association.

The Revd Mr Ripley is appointed to receive the Donations in the County of Fairfield, the Revd Mr Waterman for the County of Newhaven, the Revd Mr Day for the County of Litchfield, the Revd Mr Hinsdale for the County of Hartford, the Revd Mr Cogswell for the County of Windham, & the Revd Mr Ellis for the County New London.

The Revd Mr Williams of Northford, the Revd Mr Goodrich of Durham, & the Revd Mr Trumbull of North Haven are appointed a Committee for the purposes specified in the 3^d Article above.

The Revd Mr Taylor of New Milford, the Rev^d. Mr Waterman of Wallingford & the Revd Mr Bliss of Ellington are appointed Missionaries, any two of them to go upon the Mission as they shall agree. These Missionaries are directed to travel thro' the Settlements in the Wilderness to the Northwestward of this Colony; but not to proceed further Northward than the northern boundary of the Province of New York: where they shall judge their Services may be most likely to be beneficial; excepting so far as they shall be more particularly instructed by the Committee. — They are directed to perform all parts of the Ministerial office as Providence shall open a Door. They are directed to set out upon this Mission sometime next Spring; to spend 5 or 6 months in their Mission if the Committee are able to provide for their support so long — to keep an exact Journal of their Proceedings, & give as accurate an account as Possible of the State of the several Places they pass thro'; that the General Association may be better able to determine where to send their Missionaries in coming Time.

Voted that the following Advertisement be published in the several News Papers in this Colony —

The General Association of the Colony of Connecticut convened by adjournment at New Haven Sept 15th 1774 have appointed the following Gentlemen to Receive the Subscriptions made or that may hereafter be made for the purpose of Supporting Missionaries to be sent to the Settlements in the Wilderness to the Northwestward of this Colony, viz: the Rev^d Mr. Ripley for the County of Fairfield &c — to be by them transmitted to the Revd Messrs Warham Williams, Elizur Goodrich, & Benjamin Trumbull, who are appointed a Committee for carrying this Purpose into execution. And the several Ministers in the Colony who have rec^d or may hereafter Receive Subscriptions for this Purpose are desired to send whatever Donations they shall collect to the Gentlemen above mentioned as receivers in the Several Counties, taking their receipts for the Money delivered.

Test EBENEZAR BALDWIN, Scribe.

The association then resumed the Consideration of some proper Methods for the Revival of Discipline in our Churches. A Draught was then read before this Body for the improvement of Discipline by the Revd Mr Lockwood according to appointment. The following thoughts upon that subject are approved by this Body & recommended to the practice of the Churches.

This Association taking into consideration the great Declension of Religion & the disorderly Walk of many of its Professors & neglect of Duty in others under the Bonds of the Covenant, which is owing in a great Measure we apprehend to the want of Discipline in the Church of Christ; which is to the Dishonor of Christ the great Lawgiver to his Church & to the reproach & wounding of his Visible Disciples who are under special obligations to walk with Christ in all his Statutes & ordinances & to do whatsoever he commands them; nor can the Church in this depraved State, wherein it is impossible but that offences will come, long maintain Purity & good order where the Discipline of Christ's house is neglected; but the glory of the Church is then departed: 'tis no longer beautiful as Tirzah, comely as Jerusalem & terrible as an army with Banners; nor can it properly be said Christ rules that house where his own Laws are neglected. Altho many have desired & some attempted to recover discipline so manifestly Lost in the Churches; but with little success; which we fear will yet be the case unless it pleases God of his great mercy to pour out the Divine Spirit upon our Churches to the Revival of Religion in the power & purity of it — however Duty is ours & the Event is God's; we would therefore Reccommend it

1. As an Incumbent Duty on Ministers both in public & private, to take pains with the professed Disciples of Jesus, to convince them of the nature & end of Discipline & the necessity of maintaining it in the Church of Christ in its militant State, without which it cannot subsist in Character. They should be made sensible of the advantages of a Christian Watch over each other, whereby Every Member hath the friendly assistance of the whole community with which they are Specially connected, to prevent their Wandering, or reclaim them when they have gone astray.

2. We judge it expedient in this day of Declension & Dissoluteness for Ministers to be frequent & pressing in their addresses to Parents & heads of Families, especially such as are under the Bonds of the Covenant that the eyes of the Lord are upon them & God requires that they perform their Vows, not only for themselves but also for those committed to their care, to train them up in the Nurture & admonition of the Lord by Instructions, Councils, Reproofs & Discipline as needed &c., the neglect of which we apprehend is one cause of much Disorder both in Church & State.

3. To effect the good End proposed, we recommend it to the Churches, that all the Children of the Covenant be considered & Treated as subjects of Discipline & objects of their tender care & christian Inspection; to see that such Lambs of the Flock have the advantage of Christian Instructions & Government in their Early Days; & as such come forward in years & understanding, if they are guilty of Scandal or Neglect to take upon themselves the Bonds of the Covenant by their own act; that the Church use proper methods to reclaim them & bring them to a sense of their Duty by admonitions both private & public if need be; & in case these methods prove ineffectual to reclaim them after all due Patience hath been used; it is the Duty of the Church publicly to discharge themselves of their Watch & Care over them.

4. Because of the so great neglect of Discipline in Christ's house it appears to us men become fearless of transgressing, & that Delinquents & Scandalous Persons are often Neglected to their Damage, when they need the wholesome Discipline the great head of the Church has Instituted; That guilt often lies upon the Church by suffering Sin upon a Brother, merely because no one takes upon him the friendly part of a Complainant; for what equally concerns all is too often neglected by all.

To remedy this Disorder we propose, that each Church chuse a small number of the Brethren as a Committee of Inspection, Inquiry & Information, to act with or by direction of the Pastor, who upon hearing anything of their Members, which they apprehend to be Matter of Scandal & Church Censure are to consider themselves as under obligations to make Inquiry, examine Evidence &c, and endeavor by private measures to heal the Difficulty, reclaim offenders & restore peace & good order to the Church; But if they fail hereof & find it necessary for the Honor of God, the peace & Edification of the Church & the good of offenders, then one of the said Committee to exhibit a formal, written Complaint to the Church, & support the Charge with what Light & Evidence he can; that the Church may proceed against such offenders according to the Laws of Christ's Kingdom & be lead to a righteous Judgment. Yet this is not intended to cut off any brother from his Right of exhibiting a Charge in his own Name against an offender if he desires it, & the matter of offence renders a Charge Necessary.

The foregoing Particulars are recommended by this association to the practice of each of the several Pastors & Churches in this Colony so far as can be done with Peace & Unanimity.

The above *Voted* as the Doings of this association. Concluded with Prayer.

Test EBENEZER BALDWIN, Scribe.

NOTES.

[1]. Thomas Canfield Pastor in Roxbury from 1744 to 1795.
[2]. John Miner Pastor in South Britain from 1768 to 1790.

1775.

At a General Association of the Pastors of the consociated Churches of the Colony of Connecticut, convened by Deligation, at the House of the Revd Benjamin Throop in Norwich June 20th A D 1775

Present

The Revd Messieurs
- Elnathan Whitman
- Ephraim Little
- Benjamin Throop
- Stephen White
- Eliphalet Williams
- Elijah Sill
- Elizur Goodrich
- Simon Waterman
- Eliphalet Huntington
- Hezekiah Ripley and
- Jonathan Murdock [1].

The Revd Elnathan Whitman was chosen Moderator and Mr Goodrich Scribe.

The General Association was opened with a Sermon from Exodus III Chap. 2 Verse, by the Revd Eliphalet Huntington.

M^r. Goodrich reported the State of Matters relative to the sending of Missionaries to the Northwestward, as was proposed the last General Association, and thereon Mr Throop & Mr Williams were joined with him as a Committee to draw up and bring in a Draught of what may be proper for the General Association to do further in prosecuting the Design.

Adjourned 'till to morrow morning 7 o'Clock.   June 21.st 7 o'Clock A. M. met according to adjournment. The Committee appointed to prepare a Draught relative to the Affair of Missionaries brougt in one which was read, approved and is as follows — "The General Association being of Opinion that great and good Ends, through the Blessing of God, may be answered by sending Missionaries into the back Settlements, as was proposed the last General Association, and being unwilling that the Design should fail, tho' from the Report made by M^r. Goodrich it appears not practicable to be immediately executed, do continue the same Gentlemen who were appointed by the last General Association, as a Committee to carry the Plan into the Execution, and do recommend to the Receivers in the several Counties to collect the Monies which have been subscribed and transmit the same to the Committee with all convenient speed that they may be enabled to act in the Affair as providence shall open a Door, and if possible carry it in some Measure unto Execution this Year; otherwise they are directed to lay the matter before the next General Association.

The General Association are apprehensive that the perplexed & melancholly State of public Affairs has been a Discouragement to this Design, & a Reason why the Collections have not been brought in, as was expected; but however dark present Appearances are, they cannot but hope God will yet give Opportunity of executing the Scheme proposed, to his own Glory, and the Spread and Increase of the Redeemer's Kingdom.

At present affairs are in such a Situation that the General

Association can give no particular Directions to the Committee for the Management of the Business, but would have them use their best Discretion, having a regard to what was done by the former General Association, as nearly as Circumstances will permit: And though in the opinion of the General Association it would be best That both Missionaries should be ordained Ministers, yet if it be found impracticable to send two such, the Committee are at Liberty to send some suitable Candidate, as one, under the Direction of the other who shall be ordained.

We recommend the Matter to the serious consideration of Ministers and all good Christians, and hope they will encourage it and assist all concerned in the Execution of it; and if this be done we hope some attempt may be made before Winter.

The General Association taking into serious Consideration the destressing and melancholly State of public affairs in the British American Colonies, and the Dangers they are now threatened with from the oppressive Measures of the British Court are sensible of the loud calls of God in his Providence, that humbling ourselves under his righteous Hand, we turn unto him by unfeigned Repentance and Amendment, and we are thankful that God has put it into the Hearts of our Rulers so frequently to call upon us and our People to those Duties, that laying aside all Levity and extravagance and undue Diversions, we should be excited to earnest Prayer and Supplication, and meet with our People for that Purpose as frequently as Convenience will admit. We trust our Rulers will still encourage this good Work and strengthen the Hands of all the Ministers in it. We also rejoice that in so many of our Churches and Congregations there appears a Disposition of attending on such Seasons and wish it may become General and Universal: We look upon it in particular our Duty to stir up ourselves and all our Brethren in the Ministry to be forward in leading our People in this Day of Trouble to be calling on God, and to have special seasons of Prayer and that the whole of our Congregations be urged to attend them; This is certainly our Duty and what we are particularly directed to in the Word of God, that we answer the Messages of Heaven in Divine Providence and become an humble, penitent and pardoned People, prepared for the Divine Mercy and Salvation. And as we are the Covenant people of God, and have enjoyed the Special Privileges of the Gospel, we look upon it that God in his Providence calls upon us to consider our Covenant obligations and that it is the indispensable Duty of Ministers to impress the minds of all their People with the Duty of owning the Covenant God of our Fathers; that those who have come under explicit and personal Engagements humbling themselves for all Breaches of their Vows, should be quickened to walk with God in all his Commandments and Ordinances, and that others should be reminded of their awful Neglects and urged to remember and own the Obligations they are laid under by God's Covenant, and improve the Privileges of it, and if any Churches or Congregations shall see fit and convenient publicly and *as a body* to renew their Covenant with God we should approve it; but must leave the Matter to the Prudence of Ministers and Churches to determine particularly for Themselves; At the same Time we would solemnly Charge ourselves, our Brethren in the Ministry and our People to be earnest in seeking and turning to God, and that bringing forth such Fruits as he requires we may have tokens for good, and still trust in his fatherly Kindness, that he will appear for this Land, scatter the dreadful Cloud that is over it, secure & perpetuate all its Rights and Privileges and cause the Churches here planted to flourish so long as the Sun and Moon shall endure.

Voted that the next Meeting of the General Association on the third Tuesday of June next be at the House of the Reverend Hezekiah Gould in Cornwall, and provided it should be inconvenient for Mr Gould to entertain them that the Association of Litchfield County appoint a Place and inform the other Associations.

A true Record of the Doings of the General Association —

Test Elizur Goodrich, Scribe.

A true entry of the Record of the Doings of the General Association.

Test BENJAMIN TRUMBULL
Register of the General Association.

NOTES.

¹. Jonathan Murdock Pastor 2d Greenwich from 1774 to 1785.

1776.

At a general Association of the Pastors of the Consociated Churches of the Colony of Connecticut, convened by deligation at Cornwall in Connecticut June 18: 1776 —

Upon Motion made, it was voted that this Association will from Time to Time order to be printed and dispersed to the several Consociated Churches of this Colony whatever shall be transacted by them of general Concern to the Churches; and that when any thing is not published in this Manner, it is to be understood that nothing material of this Kind was transacted by the Association.

June 19th Voted That the preceding vote, and the Address of this Association to the Consociated Pastors and Churches of the Colony of Connecticut, with the Advice of the General Association respecting Discipline in the year 1774 be printed forthwith and distributed to the several Consociated Pastors and Churches of this Colony; And the Scribe is directed to see it done.

Truly extracted from the Minutes of the General Association.

Test EBENEZAR BALDWIN, Scribe

A true Entry of the Extracts from the Minutes of the General Association.

Test BENJAMIN TRUMBULL, Register.

N. B. The original Minutes of the General Association in 1776 being lost (probably taken and destroyed by the enemy at Turtle Bay, where the Revᵈ Mʳ Baldwin lost a considerable Number of his Manuscripts, or afterwards in their Excursion to Danbury) these Extracts, which had been preserved in the printed Address to the Consociated Pastors and Churches of the Colony of Connecticut, are registered in their proper Place, agreeable to a Vote of the General Association in June 1778, which may be seen in its Place.

An ADDRESS of the General Association to the CONSOCIATED PASTORS and CHURCHES in the Colony of Connecticut.

Reverend and *Beloved*,

Deeply impressed with a sense of the calamitous State in which our Land is involved: Reduced by the arbitrary edicts of the British Parliament, and the cruel and inhuman Methods used to inforce them to the sad Necessity of defending by Force and Arms those precious Privileges which our Fathers fled into this Wilderness quietly to enjoy: Declared Rebels by the British King and Parliament; Not only the Power of Britain, but a large Army of Foreign Mercenaries, hired at a most extravagant Price, employed to dragoon us into Obedience or rather abject Submission to Tyrrany: Our Foreign Trade almost annihilated: Many of our Towns ruined and destroyed: Our Children, our Friends, our dearest Connections called from our Bosoms to the Field of Battle; and some of them captivated and enslaved by our cruel and insulting Foes: Detestible Parricides interspersed among us, aiming to give a fatal stab to the Country which gave them birth, and hath hitherto fostered them in her indulgent Bosom: And in many Places both at home and abroad deplorable Sickness wasting away the Inhabitants of our Land: Deeply impressed with a View of these dire Calamities, we are led anxiously to enquire what Sins and Iniquities prevalent in our Land have called down these heavy Judgments of Heaven upon us: Fully assured both from sacred Writ and the usual Method of the Dispensations of God's Providence, that such Calamities are ever the effects of abounding Sin and Iniquity, and that sincere Repentance, and a thor'o Reformation is the only probable Method to avert these Tokens of Divine Wrath.

Upon serious Enquiry we find there is an awful Declension from that purity and Strictness both of Doctrine and Manners which characterized our Ancestors, whom God so signally planted, protected and defended in this Land. Many of the distinguishing Doctrines of the Gospel are treated by great Numbers not only with disregard and Neglect, but even with Contempt: Such as the Doctrines of the Sovereignty of divine Grace: Of the Necessity of a deep and thoro' Conviction of Sin, and of Conversion by the effecacious regenerating Influence of the divine Spirit: Of the necessity of internal Holiness in order to Salvation &c. But still greater is the awful Depravation of our Manners. God's Sabbaths which used in the primitive Ages of New England to be kept with a most exemplary Strictness, are now most impiously profaned: In many by slothful Absence from public Worship, or by unnecessary Travelling, Business, or Visiting on God's holy Day: In others by a careless, indolent and irreverent Attendance on public Worship; or by playful Diversions, especially of the younger Sort, even in the Time of divine Service: By spending the interims of public Worship in discoursing of public News or other secular Concerns. And the remainder of the Day, not appropriated to public Worship, instead of being spent in family Instruction and Worship, and the Duties of the Closet, is but too generally wasted away in slothful Indolence, or trifling Amusements. And so awfully is God's sacred Name profaned among us that the vices of profane Cursing and Swearing, which but lately were confined to a few despicable Wretches in our populous and trading Towns, contaminated by their Intercourse with Foreigners, have now penetrated the obscurest corners of our Country; so that even the most remote and obscure Villages will furnish each many Instances of Wretches expert in this Language of Hell: And in our Armies we have reason to fear that like a mighty Torrent it carries all before it. God's sacred Word is treated by amazing Numbers as tho' unworthy their serious Attention: Few appear anxious to found their Faith upon its sacred Truths, or conform their Practice to its divine Precepts. The means of Religion we have been so highly favored with have been greatly abused. The Gospel of Jesus Christ we have Reason to fear receives a cordial Welcome from but very few. God's Ordinances are treated by vast Numbers with Neglect, and by not a few we fear with Contempt. Great Numbers, much the greater Part of the rising Generation, tho' dedicated to God in Infancy neglect to take upon themselves the Bonds of the Covenant, which can be construed in no other Light, than a denial of Christ. As a consequence of this their Children are undevoted to God in Baptism; and much the greater Part of our Congregations turn their Backs upon the holy Ordinance of the Lord's Supper. And in many of our Churches numerous are those who are guilty of the most glaring Contradiction in that they show no Concern for the Improvement of Religion in their own Souls by attending on the Ordinance of the Lord's Supper, while they appear anxious to devote their Children to God in Baptism. The Neglect of God's Worship in Families in a very growing and fashionable Sin; and as if the Hearts of Parents were hardened against the Fruit of their own Bowels — As if destitute of natural Affection, Parental Instructions in Religion, Counsels, Warnings and Restraints seem in great Measure to cease from among us. Many gross Immoralities shockingly abound, which are become so fashionable that in the estimation of many they almost cease to be Vices. Of this kind we may reckon *Intemperance*. How many wallow in the more than bestial sin of Drunkenness, and seek every Opportunity by the immoderate Use of Strong Drink to deprive themselves of Reason that distinguishing Badge of Humanity and reduce themselves to a level with the Brutes! Almost beyond Account have been the Quantities of strong Drink annually consumed in this Colony; and the mournful Complaints under the present Scarcity, show what a wretched Influence it hath acquired over us. Uncleanness, with many Customs and practices leading thereto — Injustice — Fraud — Oppression — Extortion — Covetousness — Selfishness — A want of Love to our Country, and of a Disposition to prefer the great Interests of the Community to the little private Interests of our own — A Disposition to Anarchy while struggling for Liberty — Impatience under lawful and necessary Restraints — A boundless Freedom in censuring the Conduct and defaming the Characters of others, while that Christian Watchfulness and brotherly Reproof which the Gospel enjoins is almost fallen into disuse, and that wholesome Discipline which Christ hath appointed to be Kept up in his Church for the preventing and correcting of Immoralities seems in our Churches to be in a languishing, dying State.

And under all these Judgments and Calamities an awful Stupidity seems to prevail among all Ranks of Men: In a a great Measure insensible of the Hand of God herein, while we are venting our Resentment against and loading with Imprecations the Instruments of our Sufferings: Attending to them rather as Injuries from Man, than the righteous Corrections of an holy God, justly provoked by our Sins. So far from being led to a general Repentance and Reformation by these awful Judgments, every Species of Wickedness seems rather increasing in our Land. A Confidence of Success seems to prevail, without a proportionate Concern to remove the procuring Cause of our Afflictions. These and the like, appear to us, upon serious Enquiry, to be the prevailing Sins of our Land.

Now the Voice of Revelation and Reason conspire to warn us against entertaining Expectations of a Restoration of our former Tranquility and Happiness, unless these abounding Sins and Iniquities, the procuring Cause of these Evils, be in some Measure removed. They jointly bid us expect accumulated Miseries and Destresses, till a general Reformation take Place. They equally join to encourage our Hopes, that, upon Virtue and Religion's flourishing again, God's Hand now so heavy upon us will be removed and our former Tranquility and Happiness be restored.

Tenderly concerned (as we would hope) for both the temporal and spiritual Interests of our dear Country, and fully convinced of the Necessity of our being deeply humbled under a Sense of our Sins, and of a general Reformation's taking Place, in Order to obtain and secure these invaluable Blessings; we hope we shall obtain the serious Attention of our Brethren in the Gospel Ministry, and their and our respective Churches, While we endeavor to unite our Voice with that of our civil Fathers in bearing our Testimony against these Heaven-provoking Sins, in resolving against them, and earnestly exhorting to sincere Repentance and Reformation.

We would earnestly exhort our brethren in the Ministry, at the same time resolving the same for ourselves, to labor abundantly for the conviction of their Hearers of the prevalence of these and the like Iniquities: To urge every Argument and Motive to persuade to Repentance and Reformation; to dwell much in their preaching upon these seasonable and necessary Topics; to be painful and diligent in catechising and instructing the Children and Youth, with unremitting Importunity to call upon Parents to discharge their Duty to their dear Offspring; to use their utmost Endeavor to revive languishing Discipline; and especially by their own Example to recommend and enforce that Reformation, those Virtues and that Religion they teach the Necessity of.

We would earnestly request those to whom the Execution of our civil Laws are intrusted, to lend a helping Hand towards this necessary Reformation, by restraining open Immoralities by a due Execution of the Laws against them; especially against profane Cursing and Swearing, Sabbath-breaking and Intemperance; in which we fear there is a sinful Neglect; A vigorous Execution of the Laws may be a means to prevent the outward Deed, tho' it do not mend the Heart, and so may preserve others from the Contagion of general example. Let not such take it amiss, if we remind them that their Duty to God, their Duty to their Neighbour, and the solemn Oath they are under, do all oblige to this.

We would earnestly intreat the Professors of Religion, the

Members of our Churches, who are bound by God's sacred Covenant to a Life of Purity and Holiness, zealously to exert themselves to promote this necessary and important Work. The eyes of God and man are upon them; God expects them to lead in this Work: Their Vows, their Privileges lay them under the highest Obligations thereto. If forward in this Work, their example may have the most salutary Effects; if backward, in all Probability will be an insurmountable Obstacle. Tis to be feared that some if not most of the Sins mentioned as abounding in our Land are to be found with some of this Number. Let the guilty be exhorted to sincere Repentance and Reformation; to render their Reformation visible to those around them, that their Light may shine before others, and their Example powerfully draw them to Immitation. Let every one faithfully bear Testimony against these abounding Sins; by prudent Advice, Council, Warning and Reproof, laboring to bring others to join in this wished for Reformation. And as it lies with them principally to revive the languishing Discipline of our Churches, let them be exhorted faithfully to execute the Laws of our dear Redeemer who alone is King and Lawgiver in his Church. And as many who profess the Religion of Jesus, do as we apprehend, shamefully contradict it in their Practice, by refusing to commemorate the dying Love of our dear Redeemer, we would exhort such carefully to examine whether they have any just ground for making such a Distinction between the Ordinances of our Lord and Saviour; and whether the Practice be not a virtual Contradiction of their Profession; That they would with sincere and honest Hearts practice all the Commands of our dear Saviour and thus show forth that they are genuine Disciples of the blessed Jesus.

As the rising Generation, who are under the special Instruction, Direction and Government of their Parents, are at present an important Part of the Community, and will soon succeed in Place of those who are continually going off the Stage of action, Parents and Heads of Families have a most important Part to act in effecting (under God) this so much desired Reformation. We would therefore earnestly intreat Parents, as they regard the Interests of Religion ; as they regard the Interest and Happiness of their distressed Country ; as they have any Bowels of Compassion toward their dear and beloved Offspring ; that they would be faithful in instructing their Children and those under their Care in the Principles of Virtue and Religion — in enforcing upon them by every Argument and Motive the Practice of it ; in keeping strict Order, Regularity and Government in their Families; in councelling, warning and restraining them when needful ; that they may be educated in the Nurture and Admonition of the Lord ; that being trained up in the Ways of Religion and Virtue, they may (by God's blessing) become orderly and wholesome Members of Society, and Plants of Renown in the Vineyard of our Lord and Saviour.

And as the future Hopes both of the temporal and Spiritual Prosperity of our Country are so much founded upon the rising Generation we would be importunate with the Youth of our Churches and Congregations heartily to join in this necessary and important Work of Reformation — That they would seriously consider they have a greater Interest in the Prosperity of their Country than those more advanced in Years : That the important Betrustment now lodged with their parents of transmitting the Blessings of Religion and Liberty to Posterity will soon devolve upon them ; That they have immortal Souls bound to an Eternity of Happiness or Misery : That not only their own temporal and eternal Interests, but in some Degree also that of Thousands and Millions yet unborn will probably, in a great Degree, if not altogether, depend on the Resolution they now take, whether to join in this important Work, to renounce their Vices, Follies and Vanities and sincerely embrace & Practice the Religion of Jesus, to which they are bound by the most solemn Ties of God's Covenant, which they are laid under by Baptism : Or to continue in the Indulgence of those youthful Sins, which call down the Vengeance of Heaven upon our guilty Land :—

That they would hear the Voice of God now speaking to us in Accents of Thunder, and awake to Thoughtfulness, Seriousness and Religion.

And we would earnestly request of Ministers, of Professors, of Parents & Children, that they would one and all unite (in such Manner & so often as shall be judged best and most convenient) with penitent Hearts, to confess and deplore their Sins before Almighty God, and implore his gracious Interposition in this Day of great Calamity and Danger, to deliver us from our present Troubles, restore us to our former State of Tranquility and Happiness, and that we may be and ever continue a People to his Praise and Glory.

Signed by Order of the General Association

JOHN TRUMBULL Moderator,
Test, EBENEZER BALDWIN Scribe.

1777.

At a Meeting of the General Association of the State of Connecticut holden at Fairfield Tuesday June 17th 1777 at the House of the Rev.d Andrew Eliot —

Present —

The Reverend Messrs
- Joseph Strong
- Nathaniel Bartlet
- Robert Ross
- Hezekiah Gold [1].
- Nathan Williams [2].
- Enoch Huntington
- Andrew Eliot [3].
- Peter Starr [4].
- Samuel Wales and [5].
- Abner Benedict [6].

The Rev. Mr. Bartlet was chosen Moderator, Mr Wales Scribe. The Rev'd Robert Silliman then joined the Body.

The Preacher who had been appointed, not being present, the Rev^d Mr. Huntington was appointed in his Room.

Mr. Huntington opened the Meeting by a public religious Exercise, delivering a Sermon from Isa. 42 Chap. the three last verses.

The western Association in New London desiring the Advice of this Body with Regard to reprinting a Pamphlet giving the Reasons for which our non-conforming Progenitors dissented from the Conformists in England, the Pamphlet being read the further Consideration of it was defferred 'till tomorrow.

Adjourned till to morrow morning 8 o'clock. Wednesday Morning 8 o'clock June 18th *post Preces sederunt qui supra.*

Mr Ross and Mr Williams were appointed to make a Draught expressing the Sense of this Board with Regard to the above mentioned motion. The Draught was as follows, viz:

A Motion was from the Western Association in New London County about reprinting a Letter from some aged Nonconforming Ministers (as by the Copy of the Vote of said Association on Record may more fully appear) the general Association read over said Letter and think it very worthy to be preserved in our Churches to the latest Posterity: But inasmuch as the expense of Printing at this Time would be uncommonly great, and the attention of the Country is so much necessarily taken up about the present War; we are of opinion (for these and other weighty reasons) it will better answer the desirable ends proposed to have it printed at some future Time. And we earnestly request the said the Western Association to procure said Letter and transmit it to the Register of this Body, that it may be sent by him along with the Records to the General Association from Time to Time.

This Association then, taking into their serious Consideration the great and deplorable Neglect of the duties of Religion in general, and that important one of family Religion in particular, even in this Day of sore Rebuke, in which an holy

God is clearly testifying his high Displeasure against us, and loudly calling us to Repentance and thoro' Reformation, and a diligent earnest seeking after God in all the ways of his appointment; do therefore beg Leave to recommend to the ministers and People in this State, to exert themselves in their several Stations to encourage and promote a **Reformation** with Regard to that great Duty. As a means to that End we think the Reprinting a serious Address of Dr P. Doddridge to a Master of a Family on that subject reasonable and of public Utility: And for that end publish the following Proposals for reprinting by Subscription, said Address. It will be contained on about two sheets. For effecting the abovesaid Republication, we the Subscribers do hereby promise and engage to take off the Books we severally subscribe for, and pay the Money on the Delivery of said Books.

P. S. It is recommended to Ministers in this State to use their influence to promote the Design in the several Parishes.

M^r. Joseph Strong, Mr Huntington, Mr Williams and Mr Strong of Hartford, are appointed Managers to carry the design into Effect. The following Gentlemen are appointed to take in Subscriptions, and send them to the Managers, viz: Messrs Ross of Stratfield, Edwards of New Haven, Gold of Cornwall, Huntington of Coventry, And Silliman of Say-Brook.

N. B. If three hundred Subscribers appear the Publication not to fail.

The next General Association is appointed to be held at the House of the Revd Warham Williams in Northford on the third Tuesday in June 1778.

The above and foregoing passed as the Doings of this Association. The meeting was then concluded with Prayer by the Revd Mr Silliman at the Desire of the Moderator.

Test Samuel Wales, Scribe.

Truly registered —

Test Benjamin Trumbull,
Register.

NOTES.

1. Hezekiah Gold Jun. Pastor in Cornwall from 1755 to 1790.
2. Nathan Williams   "   in Tolland from 1760 to 1813.
3. Andrew Eliot   "   in Fairfield from 1774 to 1805.
4. Peter Starr   "   in Warren from 1772 to 1825.
5. Samuel Wales   "   in Milford from 1770 to 1782.
6. Abner Benedict   "   in Middlefield from 1771 to 1785.

1778.

At a Meeting of the General Association of the State of Connecticut June 16th 1778 — at Northford —

Present —

The Revd Messrs
- Joseph Bellamy
- Warham Williams
- Timothy Pitkin
- Nathanael Bartlet
- Nicholas Street 1.
- Nathan Williams
- Noah Wetmore
- Ammi Ruhamah Robbins
- Andrew Eliot and
- William Seward

Dr Bellamy was chosen Moderator, and Mr Eliot, Scribe.

The Association was opened with a Sermon preached by Mr Street from Rom. 13th: 11th.

Mr. Trumbull register of the general Association represented to the Body that he could not go on in the Business of his Office on account of his not being able to procure the original Manuscript of the doings of the Association in 1776 — Mr Baldwin the Scribe of said Association having departed this Life — And it was thereupon *Voted* that Mr Waterman be desired to apply to Mr Baldwin, Father of the deceased for said Manuscript — And in case it cannot be recovered Mr Trumbull is directed to record the printed Address of the above-mentioned Association to the Churches.

The Revd Aaron Kinne then joined the Body.²

It being represented to this Association that a Sum of Money subscribed for the purpose of sending Missionaries to preach the Gospel in the Settlements forming and formed to the North and Northwestward of this State, is in the hands of several Gentlemen in Continental Bills and Silver — Mr Warham Williams is hereby empowered and directed to receive and put the continental Money into the Loan Office — And Mr Benjamin Trumbull is desired to Keep the Silver money in his possession for the present.

The Revd Thomas Brockway then joined the Body.³

Voted, That it be recommended to the several Associations to send annually to the General Association a List of the Candidates for the Ministry that are licensed by them — their places of abode — and time of being licensed.

The Association then adjourned until 7 o Clock tomorrow morning.

June 17th met according to Adjournment. The Association viewing with deep Concern the growing immoralities of the present Times and the great danger our Youth and Children are in of being affected with diffusive Corruptions — do recommend to the respective Associations to consult what can be done for the Prevention of the spreading Infection among our Youth, and for the promoting of seriousness and Learning among Children in a parental way and also in our private Schools.

The Association having been informed that the Revd Mr Edwards of New Haven has transcribed a Number of his Father's Sermons, upon the Desire of Several Gentlemen in Scotland, to be printed there, and it being unlikely in the present State of Things that these Sermons can be sent to Scotland. — *Voted* to recommend it to Mr Edwards to send printed subscription papers to the several Ministers of this State in Order to procure subscriptions for a small Volume of said Sermons. And we are of Opinion that the publishing such a Volume will be of great advantage to the Interests of Religion among our People. And also hope that this will prepare the way for printing the whole of the above-mentioned discourses.

The next general Association is appointed to be at Hadam at the House of the Revd Mr May.

The above Voted unanimously to be the Doings of the Association — And the whole concluded with Prayer by the Moderator.

       Test ANDREW ELIOT Scribe

A true Entry of the Doings of the General Association
     Test BENJAMIN TRUMBULL,
            Register.

NOTES.

[1]. Nicholas Street Pastor in East Haven from 1753 to 1806.
[2]. Aaron Kinne " Groton " 1769 to 1798.
[3]. Thomas Brockway " Columbia " 1772 to 1807.

1779.

At a Meeting of the general Association of the State of Connecticut by Delegation convened at the House of the Revd Mr May in Haddam on the third Tuesday * of June AD 1779 —   Present —

The Revd Messrs {
Benjamin Pomeroy D. D.
Stephen Johnson
Robert Ross
Eleazer May [1]
Ebenezer Kellogg [2]
Simon Waterman
John Bliss [3]
Wm M. Tenant [4]
Isaac Lewis
Thomas Wells Bray [5] and
David Ely [6]
}

---

* June 15th.

The Revd Dr Pomeroy was chosen Moderator & Mr Ely Scribe. Several Gentlemen being occasionally present were invited to sit with the Association.

The Association was then opened by the Moderator with a Sermon from Isa. xvi: 4, 5, which was succeeded after an intermission of 20 Minutes by a Sermon from the Revd Mr Tennant from Dan. iii. 17, 18.

The Revd Messrs Beckwith and Kenny joined the Association.

A Motion from the West Association in New London County, was then laid before the Association by their Delegates to this effect — "Considering the dark Aspect upon our Churches in the Discouragement lying upon Candidates entering into the Ministry, and the present destress and difficulties of them that are already in office — from whence we fear these Churches may be left without Lights in the Candlestick — We instruct our Delegates to lay our Sentiments before the general Association, and join (if it be thought proper) to call a Convention of the Clergy of the State, appointing Time and place where it may be thought most convenient to deliberate upon this subject. — Two things have been upon our Mind: viz, That an Address be made to the Rulers and People of this State, showing our apprehension of the Danger, and the Propriety of some Exertions to save the Churches from Ruin. — Or that a modest, dutiful Representation be made to the Hon{bl} Assembly of this State, in their next session in October, of these our Apprehensions — praying their Honors to take the same into Consideration — and do as Wisdom may direct."

The motion was taken up, seriously considered, largely discussed. The Association then adjourned till tomorrow Morning 7 o'Clock.

Wednesday morning met according to adjournment. Resumed the motion that was under Consideration last Evening. After a full Discussion, these Questions were proposed viz: 1st Ques. Whether it be the minds of this Body that a Convention of the Clergy of this State, out of the several Associations to meet at some convenient Time & Place be called by this Body to take into Consideration the State of the Churches?— passed in the Negative.

2nd Ques. proposed, Whether it be the mind of this Body at this Session, that they make an Address to the people at large?— passed in the Affirmative. A Committee was then appointed to form an Address—The Gentlemen appointed were the Revd Mess.rs Johnson, Ross, Bray & Lewis.

The Committee appointed to prepare an Address to the people at large made their report. Their Draught was read. The Question then proposed was Whether this Board approves of the Address and order it to be printed and recommend the same to be publickly read in the several Congregations thro' the State? Passed in the Affirmative.

The next Question proposed was — Whether the next general Association should meet at Mr Williams's of Tolland? Passed in the affirmative.

A motion was made to appoint Committees to prepare Draughts for an Address to the Honble General Assembly, which they should lay before this Board at their next Meeting. It was put to vote Whether Mr Bray and Mr Waterman should be one of those Committees? Passed in the Affirmative. — Put to Vote Whether Mr Ross and Mr Tennant should be the other Committee? Passed in the Affirmative.

It was then put to Vote Whether this Board would appoint Mr Bray to correct and see printed the foregoing Address? Passed in the Affirmative. It was then voted to adjourn this Association 'till the 2nd Wednesday in September next to meet at New Haven in the College Chapelc 9 o'Clock A. M.

The foregoing was read and Voted as the Minutes of the Association.

By the Order of the Moderator, the Association was then adjourned 'till the Time, and at the place above mentioned.

Test DAVID ELY, Scribe.

NOTES.

1. Eleazar May   Pastor in Haddam 1756 to 1808.
2. Ebenezer Kellogg   "   Vernon 1762 to 1817.
3. John Bliss   "   Ellington 1764 to 1780.
4. Wm M. Tennant   "   Greenfield 1772 to 1781.
5. Thomas Wells Bray "   No. Guilford 1766 to 1808.
6. David Ely   "   Huntington 1778 to 1816.

1780.

At a meeting of the General Association of the State of Connecticut, at Tolland on the third Tuesday of June 1780*

Present

The Revd Messrs. { Samuel Lockwood
Elijah Loothroop
Robert Ross
Josiah Whitney [1]
Nathan Williams
Andrew Storrs
Joseph Huntington
Theodore Hinsdale
Elisha Rexford [2]
William Seward }

The Revd Mr Lockwood was chosen Moderator and Joseph Huntington Scribe.

The Association was opened with prayer by the Revd Mr Ross and a Sermon by the Revd Mr Hinsdale, for which thanks were in form returned by the body.

A motion was then made by the Delegates from Windham County in favor of the promotion of Family religion, public renewal of Covenant with God &c. as contained in a Writing bearing date May 16th 1780.

This Association having duly considered the lamentable

---

* June 20th.

declention which appears among the people of God, both in doctrine, manners and discipline do earnestly recommend that each particular association, or the ministers thereof, in smaller districts, as shall be by them deemed most convenient, speedily convene together for the purpose of solemn fasting and prayer to Almighty God for themselves, their people and for the inhabitants of the Land, in this day of abounding iniquity under the awful Judgments of the Most High; and to bewail before him the manifold abominations, whereby we have provoked his holy and awful indignation ; to humble themselves in his presence, and, as in dust and ashes, implore his mercy for his people : — That for his own name sake, and for the displays of his own glory, he would be pleased to visit all the inhabitants of the Land with the effecacious energy of his holy spirit, that true religion may universally revive in the power and glory of it, and that all our abounding vices and immoralities may be effectually suppressed.

We further advise, that each particular association do, as shall appear to them most proper and becoming stir up themselves and one another, and address all, ages and characters of people under their spiritual watch and care in such a solemn and particular manner, as shall appear to them best adapted for the awakening, instruction, and reformation of this stupid and backsliding generation : — That they earnestly exhort every one to forsake their sins and turn to the God of their Fathers and prepare to meet Him with unfeigned repentance, holy submission, and an intire dedication of themselves to him, now he is coming out against us in the terrors of his Wrath, and not meeting us as a man.

We do also judge it is agreeable with the Will of heaven, at this day, that, according to the frequent practice of the people of God, in ages past, and which he has always approved by gracious Manifestations of acceptance, the ministers of the Gospel do call on the people of their charge, by fasting and prayer to humble themselves under the mighty hand of

God, to put away all their sins and openly, explicitly an speedily to acknowledge as the God of their Fathers, and their God, in that relation, in which they respectively stand, whether as those who have openly avouched the Lord Jehovah as their God and everlasting Portion, and that eat and drink with Christ at his sacred Table, or as those who have received the ordinance of Baptism for themselves and children ; or if they are only distinguished from the nations that know not God, by having their lot in a valley of Vision, and under the glorious light of the Gospel and calls of redeeming love : — That all may know the bonds of God that are upon them respectively, and be sensible how much he reasonably requires of them, in grateful and dutiful returns for all his benefits.

We do also advise that each association and each minister of the Gospel, in particular, with becoming zeal for the honor of Christ, and the good of his people exert themselves for the revival of discipline in the Church, watching over each other in love, and striving together according to the rules of the Gospel, that all who have the vows of God upon them may know and regard their Duty in all things : — And, that all labor for those things that in the Way of pure religion make for peace, that the God of peace may return to us, in his great mercy and dwell with us, as the Glory of his people in the midst of them, and be our almighty protector, as a Wall of fire about us on every side.

Considering that several pastors and Churches in diverse parts of the Land, with whom we have been united in the bonds of christian and ministerial fellowship have of late gone into practices whose direct tendency is sensibly to wound the tender ties of Charity which have connected us together, and bring on a disunion, particularly in refusing intercourse of ministerial Labors, and to receive our members, on recommendation from the pastors and churches to which they belonged, to their Communion, without a particular and personal examination.

This association think ourselves called upon to declare that we view those practices of our dearly beloved brethren and their Churches with deep concern and grief, as we deem the differences on which they proceed, as by no means sufficient to render a separation between us either necessary or warrantable, and that we are ready notwithstanding to receive them in the Lord and to the utmost of our power and Opportunity to cultivate harmony and Communion with them in all things wherein we are or may be agreed, and to endeavour a removal of our unhappy differences, in due time, in that Spirit of meekness, humility, prudence and moderation which the gospel requires, or if that should be found impracticable, to bear and conduct our differences in the same spirit.

And we do earnestly recommend it to our brethren of the several associations to cultivate the same spirit and walk in the same Line of prudent Christian Conduct towards those well meaning, but as we apprehend over scrupulous, though still beloved ministers and churches, who have adopted the above mentioned grievous practices.

Voted that the Scribe be desired to make public this Clause in the result as opportunity may present.

Voted that Messrs Rowland of Windsor and Strong of Symsbury be recommended by the Moderator or Scribe in the name of this association to go and preach the Gospel to those who are destitute of it in the State of Vermont, so called, and parts adjacent.

Voted that the next general Association be at the House of the Revd Mr Stone of Lebanon.

Signed by order of the Association

JOSEPH HUNTINGTON, Scribe.

NOTES.

[1]. Josiah Whitney Pastor in Brooklyn 1756 to 1812.
[2]. Elisha Rexford   "   Monroe   1765 to 1808.

1781.

At a meeting of the General Association of the State of Connecticut, convened by delegation at the house of the Rev.^d M^r. Stone of Goshen, in Lebanon Tuesday June the 19th 1781

Present

The Revd Messrs.
- Ephraim Little
- Benjamin Pomeroy
- Benjamin Throop
- Jeremiah Day [1]
- Benjamin Dunning
- Timothy Stone [2].
- Samuel Eells [3].
- Thomas Wells Bray
- Jonathan Murdock

and produced attested certificates of their appointment.

Mr. Little was chosen moderator and Mr Bray was chosen Scribe.

The association was opened with prayer by moderator. The preacher appointed being necessarily detained, Voted, That Mr Day be desired to preach. Adjourned for public worship. A Sermon was preached by Mr Day from John 17: 21, 22, 23^{vs}. The Revd Joel Benedict joined the Association. Adjourned till 7 o'Clock tomorrow morning.

Wednesday June 20th. Met according to adjournment. Ordered that an address be drawn up to our brethren in the ministry which is as followeth.

This association taking into consideration the duty of prayer as very suitable and important for God's people at all times, but especially when the daughter of Zion is covered with a Cloud as at the present day, and that special, united and earnest prayer, with perseverance in it is both our great privilege and duty when under peculiar and trying dispensations of divine providence; do cheerfully unite and engage for ourselves, and most seriously recommend to all our

Brethren in the ministry, through this State, to stir up themselves and the people of their respective charges to fervency and perseverance in prayer. Especially that they would lead the way and use their influence with their respective congregations to set apart weekly some little portion of Time for special prayer to our covenant God; That he would gloriously display himself for the deliverance of this people, and for the building up and prosperity of Zion. We should think that as great a Union as may be, respecting the time of this duty might be very suitable; and would recommend a general Rule, Wednesday of each week a little before evening. But leaving our Brethren to choose for themselves as to the time, and the frequency of it, we do with affection and earnestness recommend the duty itself. We ought always to pray and not to faint. Have we not peculiar reasons for special prayer at this day? Have we not all possible encouragement to the sweet and precious duty from every manifestation of our gracious God? Has the great Head of the Church in past times been a Wilderness and a land of drought unto his people? O let us never say unto him in heart or in conduct, we will come no more unto thee.

Voted that copies of this address be sent out from this association to our several brethren in the ministry through the State, and that all or any of them be desired to assist us in this matter as they shall have opportunity.

Voted that the next general association be at the house of the Rev^d M^r of Ripton, in Stratford on the third Tuesday in June next. concluded with prayer.

True minutes of the Association —

Attest THOMAS WELLS BRAY, Scribe.

NOTES.

1.	Jeremiah Day	Pastor	New Preston	1770–1806.
2.	Timothy Stone	"	Goshen, Lebanon	1767–1797.
3.	Samuel Eells	"	No. Brandford	1769–1808.
4.	Joel Benedict	"	Lisbon	1770–1781.
			Plainfield	1784–1816.

1782.

At a meeting of the General Association of the State of Connecticut, at the house of the Revd David Ely in Ripton June 18th A. D. 1782

Present Revd Messrs
- Samuel Newell
- Hezekiah Gold
- Cotton M. Smith
- Richard Ely [1].
- Noah Williston [2].
- Andrew Eliot
- Elisha Rexford
- Cyprian Strong
- Isaac Lewis
- Thomas Minor [3].
- David Ely

The Revd Samuel Newell was chosen Moderator and Cyprian Strong Scribe.

The association was opened by a Sermon from Isaiah 62: 6, 7 preached by the Revd Elisha Rexford.

The Revd Messrs. Timothy Stone and Thomas Brockway joined this Body.

At the same Meeting Voted That whereas it is thought expedient by this association, that an alteration should take place as to the time of the sessions of this Body, that it be recommended to each particular association to instruct their Delegates to the next General association, as to the Time; particularly as to the propriety and expediency of altering the time of its Session from the third Tuesday in June to the last Tuesday in September.

The association was adjourned till 7 o'Clock tomorrow morning. The association met according to adjournment.

The Question was put to this association — Whether ministers of the Gospel have a right, by civil Law, to recover their salaries or stipulated support?

Voted in the affirmative.

At the same time voted That it be recommended to each particular association, annually to return to the general association an account of the number of the Candidates they have licensed in their several districts, and of those who are acting under their license.

Voted, That the next general association be held at the house of the Revd Mr Johnson in Lyme.

The following is a return made to the general Association of the Candidates in the State.

Candidate	Association
Mr Lockwood	In Hartford South Association
Mr Plum	
Mr Miller	
Mr Mills	
Mr Ed^d Mills	Litchfield Association
Mr Mitchell	
Mr Bell	
Mr Everet	
Mr Parmale	
Mr Joshua Perry	Fairfield East
Mr Lankton	New Haven Association
Mr Hotchkiss	
Mr Austin	
Mr Ely	
Mr Cook	
Mr Rogers	
Mr Barnet	
Mr Baldwin	
Mr Barlow	
Mr Prudden	
Mr. Fowler	Windham Association
M^r. Lyon	
Mr Hyde	Hartford North
Mr Ely	

N. B. The doings of Association entered above are not attested by the Scribe, as may appear by the original on file, but was by him enclosed in a Letter to the Register as a Record of the doings of said Association, and is truly entered.

Test BENJAMIN TRUMBULL, Register
of the General Association.

NOTES.

¹. Richard Ely — Pastor — No. Madison — 1757-1785.
². Noah Williston — West Haven — 1760-1811.
³. Thomas Miner — Westfield — 1773-1820.

1783.

The General Association of the State of Connecticut met at the House of the Rev^derend Mr Johnson in Lyme on the 17th Day of June AD 1783

Present —

The Reverend Messieurs
- James Cogswell
- Stephen Johnson
- Warham Williams
- Cotton Mather Smith
- Josiah Whitney
- Eleazer May
- Elizur Goodrich
- Theodore Hinsdale
- Elijah Parsons (¹.)
- David Ely and
- Nathan Perkins (².)

The Reverend Mr Cogswell was chosen Moderator, and Mr Goodrich was chosen Scribe.

The Association was opened with prayer offered by the moderator.

The Reverend Mr Dunning, who was appointed to preach on the occasion, being absent, the Revd Mr Whitney was desired to perform that Service.

The General Association took into consideration the proposed alteration of the time of its meeting, and having heard the opinion and sentiments of the several particular Associations, as communicated by the members present, this association is unanimously of the opinion, that an alteration of the time of its meeting is inexpedient and therefore that the General Association shall continue to meet on the Third Tuesday of June as usual.

The Rev^d. M^r. Aaron Kinne joined the association.

Voted unanimously, That it be recommended to the particular associations that the Recommendations of Candidates for preaching the Gospel be limited for the space of four years, and that the limitation be expressed in the recommendation, and provided the candidates shall not be settled in the ministry within that term, and yet still aim to continue in the business of preaching, that they apply for a renewal of their recommendation, either to the association which gave them the former recommendation, or to that in which they mostly reside.

The following questions were proposed to this association by the Eastern association in New London County.

1st. What is the duty of ministers when invited to sit in council with separate preachers to advise in matters respecting a union between Brethren of the standing churches and those of the separate preachers?

2. Is it matter of duty and expediency to introduce any of the separate preachers into the ministry if they will submit to regular Ordination?

3. What shall be done respecting our destitute Churches and congregations whose resettlement in the enjoyment of gospel ordinances is improbable?

The General Association having considered these Questions is unanimously of opinion in respect of the first Question, That regular ministers should not set in council with separate preachers in any such form as shall expressly or constructively approve or own such separate preachers, in the character of ministers properly authorized according to the gospel constitution.

In regard to the second Question, the general association

is unanimously of the opinion that however there may possibly be cases in which those who have been separate preachers, on proper application being found on trial and examination by some regular association, or by a council of regular ministers and churches, to renounce their separatical principles and practices and to be otherwise qualified may be admitted to regular ordination, yet considering the dangerous nature and pernicious effects of those principles and practices, if any of those preachers are ever admitted to regular ordination it ought to be done with great caution, and not until such preachers have reconciled themselves to the churches from which they have separated, which is therefore earnestly recommended to the several associations in all such cases as may arise, and to all councils who may be concerned in them.

The General Association in consideration of the third Question unanimously recommend to the several Associations in which such vacant churches and congregations are found to afford them all the assistance they can with convenience, especially by preaching frequent Lectures among them, and administering the ordinances of the gospel as often as may be.

At the same time the General association earnestly recommend to all such churches and congregations the most serious attention to their State and the awful danger they are in of exposing themselves to the displeasure of the great Head and King of the Church, while they live destitute of a settled gospel ministry and ordinances, and without taking suitable pains to enjoy them, and that they be exhorted to use all proper means to resettle the gospel ministry : and the particular associations are desired to notify this recommendation to such vacant churches and join their recommendation to this. The General Association is further of Opinion that the matter is of so great and serious importance as to require the attention of ministers and people in general ; and therefore the general Association appoint the Reverend Messieurs Cotton Mather Smith, Robert Ross, Eleazer May, John Devotion, Theodore Hinsdale, Levi Hart, Timothy Stone, Isaac Lewis and Samuel Walls a committee to consider the matter at large. The Committee is desired to obtain the best advice they can of ministers and other Gentlemen of Character in this State, as to what further measures may be expedient, and make report to the next General Association.

The first meeting of the Committee is appointed to be at Yale College in New Haven the day after Commencement at 9 oClock in the morning.

The next General Association is appointed to meet at the House of the Revd Samuel John Mills in Torringford in the County of Litchfield at 11 oClock in the Forenoon of the third Tuesday of June next.

A true Record of the Doings of the General Association.

Test ELIZUR GOODRICH, Scribe.

NOTES.

[1]. Elijah Parsons Pastor East Haddam 1772–1816.
[2]. Nathan Perkins "   West Hartford 1772–1833.

1784.

At a meeting of the General Association in the State of Connecticut, convened at the house of the Revd Mr Mills in Torringford on the third Tuesday in June 1784*

Present

Revd Mess'rs Jonathan Mash[1] and Timothy Pitkin, from the North Association in Hartford County, Andrew Stores from the Association in New Haven County, John Smalley and Abner Benedict from the south association in the County of Hartford, Jeremiah Day and Samuel Mills, from the Association in the County of Litchfield, Justus Mitchell[2] from the western association in Fairfield County, Henry Ely[3] from the western association in the County of New London, Samuel Nott[4] from the eastern Association in the County of New London.

Revd Mr Pitkin was chosen moderator of the General Association.

Mr Justus Mitchell was chosen Scribe.

---

* June 15th.

The association was opened by the public service performed by Mr Day.

A report of the Committee appointed by the last General Association, to attend to the state of destitute churches, was laid before this association, and after an amendment was adopted, as follows.

A Committee having been appointed by this Body at their last Session to take into consideration the condition of the destitute Churches in this State, in order to their supply; and said Committee having reported what appeared to them the most eligible method of treating those destitute *Churches*, which neglect a becoming care for the enjoyment of Gospel ordinances, and their resettlement among them.

On hearing the report of said Committee, this association, after deliberating and conversing largely upon the subject, is of opinion, that in cases where there may be reason to apprehend a faulty neglect of proper endeavours, in any destitute Church to settle a minister over them in the Lord, it is the duty of those pastors, who are in the vicinity, to take with them some respectable characters from among the brethren of their churches, and obtain a Conference with the members of such destitute church, and in a candid Christian manner enquire into the causes of their neglect; and if they shall find them guilty of censurable negligence, to inculcate upon them the importance of gospel ordinances, and (if possible) to persuade them to pay a proper attention to the matter, and if such measures should prove ineffectual, and said Church continue criminally negligent, after due pains taken, that it is the duty of such neighbouring pastors and brethren, to exhibit a complaint against such church to the moderator of the Consociation to which it belongs, if consociated, that it may be dealt with as walking disorderly, and cut off from the Body if irreclaimable; and if said church be unconsociated that it is the duty of the churches in communion with it to withdraw communion from it, if found pertinaciously offending against the Laws of Christ in the above particular. But that those individuals of such offending Church, as appear disposed to walk orderly, if any such there be, ought to be taken under the protection of neighboring sister Churches, or the consociation, if consociated.

The association adjourned till seven o'clock tomorrow morning. The Association met according to adjournment. The Scribe was appointed to transcribe the report, and send one to each association in this State.

The next General Association is appointed to be attended on the third Tuesday in June next, at the House of M^r. Samuel Nott, in the 2^d Society of Norwich, and eastern Association in the County of New London.

Test JUSTUS MITCHELL, Scribe.

NOTES.

[1]. Jonathan Marsh Pastor in New Hartford from 1739–1794.
[2]. Justus Mitchell   "   " New Canaan   "   1783–1806.
[3]. Henry Ely   "   " Killingworth   "   1782–1801.
[4]. Samuel Nott   "   " Franklin   "   1782–1849.

1785.

At a meeting of the General Association of the ministers of the State of Connecticut at the house of the Revd Samuel Nott in Norwich on the third Tuesday in June 1785*

Present —

Reverend Messieurs
{
James Cogswell, Moderator
Josiah Whitney, Scribe
Richard Ely
George Colton [1].
Enoch Huntington
Ammi Ruhamah Robbins
Levi Hart
Theodore Hinsdale
Thomas Wells Bray
John Avery [2].
Samuel Nott
Stephen Williams Stebbins [3].
}

* June 21.

The Association was opened with prayer by the moderator. Upon representation that the Lecture the day after Commencement at New Haven is not attended upon by ministers in general and thereby the design thereof is much frustrated, the opinion of this association is asked, whether it is advisable said Lecture be continued ? This Association taking into consideration the general design thereof, are unwilling it should be discontinued; therefore would earnestly recommend it to the particular Associations to desire those of their Body who may attend Commencements, not to suffer any little inconvenience to prevent their attendance upon a service peculiarly designed for their profit; lest they give occasion to its being said that ministers are as unmindful of obligations to attend religious services as others.

The following questions were proposed to the Association.

1. Whether the practice of inviting young Gentlemen to preach, and recommending them to the Work of the ministry before they have been examined and approved by Associations or their Committee be regular?

Voted in the Negative.

2. Whether the late Ordination of one Mr Day at Killingly performed by Messrs Cleveland, Bradford, Snow, Park and Spalding ought to be acknowledged regular? Voted in the negative.

Resolved by this Body, that the practice of marrying persons not having their intentions of marriage published as the law directs is irregular and of pernitious tendency; and trust that ministers will not join any in marriage before they have observed the steps of the law in this matter.

This Association taking into consideration the great duty and importance of having the interpositions of providence in the events that have effected and attended the late American Revolution, religiously improved, not only by present but future generations, and that some suitable and concise history be prepared for that purpose; accordingly request the following Gentlemen viz: Revd Messrs Enoch Huntington, Benjamin Trumbull, Levi Hart, Theodore Hinsdale and Thomas

Wells Bray to collect and compile such a history; and that the Revd Mr Trumbull in particular be desired to digest and write the whole and prepare it for the press.

Voted that the next General Association be at the House of the Revd Dr Goodrich at Durham.

Signed by order of the Association,

JOSIAH WHITING, Scribe.

NOTES.

[1]. George Colton   Pastor in Bolton   from 1763–1812.
[2]. John S. Avery   "   Stamford   "   1779–1791.
[3]. Stephen W. Stebbins "   Stratford   "   1784–1813.

1786.

At a meeting of the General Association of the State of Connecticut at the House of the Revd Elizur Goodrich D.D. in Durham June 20th A. D. 1786

Present

Reverend Messieurs
- Joseph Bellamy D.D.
- Stephen Johnson
- Robert Ross
- Josiah Whitney
- Elizur Goodrich D.D.
- John Devotion
- Benjamin Boardman
- Enoch Huntington
- Jonathan Edwards D.D. [1].
- Nathan Perkins
- Noah Merwin [2].
- Samuel Nott and
- Nathan Fenn [3].

The Reverend Dr Joseph Bellamy was chosen Moderator, and Enoch Huntington, Scribe. The Association was opened with prayer and a Sermon by the Reverend Dr Edwards from

1 Cor. 1: 30. For in him are ye in Christ Jesus, who of God is made unto us — Righteousness.

Voted by this Association, that the Reverend Mr Benjamin Trumbull be desired to proceed in the compilation of the History which he, together with others, was desired by the last General Association to form, in commemoration and for the serious improvement of the events attending the late American Revolution; and that Messieurs Robert Ross and Enoch Huntington inform him of this desire of the present General Association, and afford him their advice and assistance in carrying this desire into execution.

This Association received of the Reverend Benjamin Trumbull four pounds ten shillings and six pence half penny, lawful money, which he had in his hands, belonging to the General Association, which money the Reverend Warham Williams was desired to Receive and Keep until called for by the Association, and accordingly it was committed to his Trust. Afterwards the same money was Voted to be given to the Reverend Isaac Lewis, late of Wilton, provided he shall be inclined to spend as many as five Sabbaths in preaching and administering Gospel Ordinances in any of the New-formed or forming Settlements that are destitute; and that the Reverend Dr Bellamy receive the aforesaid money, and give the same to Mr Lewis, upon his complying with the beforementioned condition.

The list of preaching Candidates brought in to this Association from the several particular Associations is as followeth — viz:

Litchfield County,

Messieurs Adoniram Judson, Edmund Mills.

New Haven.

Messieurs Levi Lankton, Medad Rogers, Jonathan Maltby, Jabez H. Tomlison, Lemuel Tyler, Walter King, Samuel Goodrich, Jedidiah Morse, Payson Williston, Thomas Holt.

Hartford County, North Association,

Messieurs Allen Olcott, Ebenezer Kingsbury.

South Association

Messieurs Wait Cornwall, Ethan Osborn, David Higgins, Ozias Eells, Timothy Lankton, and Samuel Mills.

Windham County

Messieurs Samuel Austin, Stephen Williams, Taylor.

New London County, East Association.

Messieurs Foster, Wilder, Page, Pierce, Andrews, Ralph.

West Association — None.

Fairfield County — None.

The Reverend Robert Ross was appointed by this General Association to preach the Conscio ad Clerum, the Day after the next Commencement at Yale College.

Voted — That the next General Association be at the house of the Reverend John Smalley in Berlin.

Voted that this Association will encourage the printing of the History which Mr. Trumbull is desired to compile, by assisting in procuring subscriptions, which it is to be hoped may be to an Amount not only sufficient to pay the printing, but also to afford some reward to Mr Trumbull for his labors and Service.

At this Association it was proposed that the following Questions should be transmitted by the Delegates to their respective Associations for their Consideration, and that the delegates to the next General Association should come prepared to offer their sentiments in the discussion of these Points.

1. In what case the dissolution of the Marriage Relation, by what is called a Divorce, may properly and allowedly take place according to the Scriptures.

2. Who was the person that appeared to Moses in the burning Bush.

3. What proof of the Truth of divine Revelation can arise from Miracles said to be wrought in Attestation of it?

Test ENOCH HUNTINGTON, Scribe.

NOTES.

¹. Jonathan Edwards Pastor New Haven North from 1769–1795.
². Noah Merwin Pastor Washington from 1785–1795.
³. Nathan Fenn " Berlin " 1780–1799.

1787.

At a General Association of the State of Connecticut convened at the House of the Reverened John Smalley in Berlin June 19th 1787

Present —

The Revd Messrs
- John Smalley
- Benjamin Trumbull
- Levi Hart
- Theodore Hinsdale
- Samuel Camp (¹.)
- Samuel John Mills
- Samuel Wales D. D. (².)
- Achilles Mansfield (³.)
- Nathan Perkins
- Moses Cook Welch (⁴.)
- Joshua Johnson (⁵.)
- Justus Mitchel and
- Frederick William Hotchkiss (⁶.)

The Reverend John Smalley was chosen moderator and Mr Benjamin Trumbull was chosen Scribe.

The Reverened Mr Lewis who was appointed to preach the Sermon before the Association being absent, Mr Trumbull was appointed to preach, who opened the Association with prayer and a Sermon from Josh. 24 : 15 — " Choose you this day whom ye will serve."

The Revd Uriel Gridley came in and joined the Association.

The Questions proposed the last General Association were discussed. Voted that the 1st Question respecting Divorce be deferred to the next General Association for further discussion.

Voted also That the 3ᵈ Question proposed the last Year respecting miracles be deferred to the next General Association for the same purpose.

The Revᵈ Dʳ Bellamy returned to this Association by the hand of the Reverend Uriel Gridley, Four Pounds Ten Shillings and Six pence half Penny, which the Dʳ had received of the General Association the last year.

Voted that the next General Association be at the House of the Reverend Nathan Perkins in West Hartford the third Tuesday in June next.

Voted that it be a standing rule That the preacher of the *Conscio ad Clerum*, at Yale College, the day after Commencement be appointed in that Association where the General Association shall set the preceding June.

Voted that the Reverend John Smalley be appointed to preach the Sermon the day after the next Commencement.

Voted that the Reverend Cyprian Strong be appointed as second in case of the Failure of the Reverend Mʳ Smalley.

Voted That the Money returned by Dʳ Bellamy be committed to the custody of Mr. Trumbull.

The List of Candidates from the Several Counties brought into the Association is as followeth.

Hartford County.

North Association Messieurs
- Joseph Kingsbury
- John Ellsworth

South Association Messieurs
- Wait Cornwall
- Ethel Orsborn
- David Higgins
- Calvin White

New Haven County.

Messieurs
- John Robinson
- Lemuel Tyler
- Payson Williston
- Thomas Holt
- Samuel Perkins
- David Hale
- Isaac Clinton
- Aaron Cook Collins.

Fairfield County.

Eastern Association   None.
Western Association   None.

New London County.

Western Association   None.

Eastern Association Messieurs
- John Wilder
- Christopher Page
- Aaron Woodworth and
- Elijah Parish

Windham County.

Messieurs
- Stephen Williams
- John Taylor
- Jonathan Ellis

Litchfield County. None.

A true Record of the doings of the General Association.

Test BENJAMIN TRUMBULL, Scribe.

NOTES.

[1]. Samuel Camp Pastor in Ridgebury from 1769 to 1804.
[2]. Samuel Wales   "   Yale College from 1782 to 1794.
[3]. Achilles Mansfield Pastor in Clinton   "   1779 " 1814.
[4]. Moses Cook Welch   "   North Mansfield from 1784 to 1824.
[5]. Joshua Johnson Pastor in East Woodstock from 1780 to 1790.
[6]. Frederick W. Hotchkiss Pastor in Old Saybrook from 1783 to 1838.

1788.

At a meeting of the General Association of the State of Connecticut at the House of the Revd Nathan Perkins in West Hartford June 17th A. D. 1788

Present

The Revd Messrs {
Nathaniel Taylor
John Willard
Cotton M. Smith
Joseph Huntington
Cyprian Strong
Thomas W. Bray
Jonathan Edwards
Nathan Perkins
Jonathan Murdock
Benoni Upson ('.)
Roswell Cook (².)
Zebulon Ely (³.)
William Lyman (⁴.)
}

The Revd Nathaniel Taylor was chosen Moderator, and Mr Cyprian Strong Scribe.

The Revd Mr Backus was appointed to preach the Conscio ad Clerum, at the Commencement in New Haven in September next.

The Revd Mr Dwight and Mr Smith joined the Association.

The Revd Messrs Jonathan Edwards, Timothy Dwight, Joseph Huntington and Cotton M. Smith were appointed a Committee to take into consideration the address of the Association of the Western District in New Haven County, respecting the State and Circumstances of the New Settlements in the States of Vermont and New York, with respect to the preaching of the Gospel, and the necessity of there being some measures taken to send suitable missionaries to preach the gospel, gather churches, and administer Gospel ordinances among them, and to report what is proper to be done thereon.

The Association was opened with a sermon from Levit. 19: 17 preached by the Revd Mr Willard. A request from the Association of Windham County was laid before this Association, requesting that some suitable Testimony might be borne against a sinful Omission in the late federal convention, in not looking to God for direction, and of omitting the mention of the name of God in the Constitution they proposed to the People for their approbation.

The Association after conversing largely upon it, laid it over till tomorrow morning for further consideration.

The Association then resumed the Discussion of the first Question referred to them from the last General Association, viz: In what case a Dissolution of the marriage Relation, by what is called a Divorce may properly and allowably take place according to the Scripture?

The Association adjourned till five o'Clock tomorrow morning.

Met according to Adjournment.

The Committee appointed yesterday made their report, which was voted and directed to be printed under the direction of Mr Perkins, under the Signature of the Moderator and Scribe of this Association.

The Association resumed the discussion of the Question under consideration the last Evening relative to Divorces.

The Association gave it as their opinion That Incontinency is the only justifiable reason for a divorce.

Voted, that Doct.^rs Goodrich, Edwards and Wales be a Committee to prepare a Draught of an Address and Petition to the General Assembly on the Subject of Divorces, and lay it before this Association on their adjournment hereafter determined.

On motion made by the Association in the western District of New Haven County, the Association Voted that the Slave Trade be unjust, and that every justifiable measure ought to be taken to suppress it.

Voted, also, that Doct^rs Goodrich, Edwards and Wales be a Committee to draw up an address and petition to the General Assembly, that some effectual Laws may be made for the total abolition of the Slave Trade, to be laid before this body at their adjournment hereafter determined :

Voted that the Address of Windham County be laid over to a future day.

A Scheme of an Union of the Presbyterians in America was presented to this Association, for their consideration, by the Association in the County of Fairfield. After deliberating upon it, Voted that it be recommended to the Consideration and Approbation of each of the particular Associations in this State.

At the request of the North Association in Hartford County, representing the great, general, and increasing neglect there is in attending to the public Worship of God — the Association Voted Messieurs Timothy Dwight & Benoni Upson be a Committee to make a draught of an Exhortation on the subject, to be publicly read, in the various Congregations, through the State.

The List of Candidates from the Several Counties, brought in to the Association is as followeth.

Litchfield Association = Edmund Mills.

Hartford North = { Ebenezer Kingsbury, John Ellsworth

Hartford South { Wait Cornwell, Ethiel Orsborn, William F. Miller, Calvin White, Elijah Gridley, Sylvester Sage.

Windham Association { Stephen Williams, John Taylor, Jonathan Ellis, Hendric Dow.

New Haven Association

John Robinson, Lemuel Tyler, Payson Williston, Thomas Holt, Samuel Perkins, David Hale, Aaron Cook Collins, Levi Lankton, William Stone, Reuben Hitchcock, Ebenezer Fitch.

New London Eastern Association —

John Wilder, Christopher Page, Hezekiah Nath' Woodruff, Asahel Huntington.

Fairfield Eastern — None.

Fairfield Western — None.
Middlesex Association = John Ely.

Voted that the next General Association be at the House of the Rev. Thomas Brockway in Lebanon.

The Committee to draw up an Address to the various Congregations on the Importance of a religious Attendance on the Duties of the Sabbath made their report which was accepted; and Doct.rs Edwards and Dwight were appointed to prepare the same for and forward it to the press with the signature of the moderator and Scribe of this Association.

The following questions were read and Voted to be offered to each particular Association for discussion viz:

1st. Is it an Institution of the Gospel that baptized Children, as soon as they are capable of eating and behaving with decency, should partake of the Lord's Supper?

2d. Are there any absolute Promises of either temporal or spiritual good, made in Scripture to the Children of Believers?

Voted that this Association be adjourned to the Day previous to Commencement, to meet in the Chapel at New Haven at 4 o'Clock in the Afternoon.

The above passed and Voted by the Association —

Test CYPRIAN STRONG, Scribe.

At a meeting of the General Association of the State of Connecticut, held by adjournment at the College Chapel in New Haven, Sept. 9th A. D. 1788

Present Rev.d Mess.rs
- Nathaniel Taylor
- John Willard
- Elizur Goodrich
- Cyprian Strong
- Thomas W. Bray
- Jonathan Edwards
- Jonathan Murdock
- Benoni Upson
- Zebulon Ely
- William Lyman

The Association was opened with prayer offered by the moderator.

The minutes of the last Association were read. Two Draughts of an Address to the General Assembly were read to the Association — one by D^r. Goodrich — the other by D^r. Edwards, to both of which objections were offered. After much conversation relative to the mode of addressing or framing a memorial to the General Assembly, relative to Divorces it was voted — That said Memorial should be predicated in part on the opinion of the association as manifested in their June Session relative to Divorces, And Doc^{tor} Edwards, M^r. Bray and Doctor Dwight were chosen a Committee to prepare a Draught of such a Memorial to be laid before the Association for their Approbation.

The Association was then adjourned till tomorrow immediately after the public Exercises of Commencement are finished, to meet at the Room of Mr Fitch.

The Association met according to adjournment. M^r. Ross joined the Body.

The committee appointed yesterday made a draught of a petition, &c., which was accepted, and one for the Total Abolition of the Slave Trade, connected with it.

Doctors Edwards and Wales were appointed a committee to forward said Petition to the General Assembly at their Session in October next.

Whereas in the minutes of the Doings of this Association in June last it is entered, that a Request was made from Windham Association, that some suitable Testimony might be borne &c., it now appears that it was not made by said Association; Voted that said Application be dismissed.

The above-voted by Association,
                    Test CYPRIAN STRONG, Scribe.

NOTES.

[1]. Benoni Upson Pastor in Kensington from 1779 to 1816.
[2]. Roswell Cook   "   " Montville   "   1784 to 1798.
[3]. Zebulon Ely   "   " Lebanon   "   1782 to 1824.
[4]. William Lyman   "   " Millington   "   1787 to 1823.

1789.

At a Meeting of the General Association of the State of Connecticut at the house of the Revd Thomas Brockway in Lebanon June 16th 1789

Present

The Revd Messrs
- Samuel Lockwood
- Elijah Lathrop
- Robert Ross
- Nathan Williams
- Benjamin Trumbull
- Timothy Stone
- Aaron Kinne
- Peter Starr
- Thomas Brockway
- Elijah Parsons
- Charles Backus (1.)
- William Seward
- Noah Merwin
- Wm Lockwood (2.)
- Joseph Vaill (3.)
- John Noyes (4.)
- Samuel Nott
- Jason Atwater (5.)

The Revd Samuel Lockwood was chosen Moderator, & Wm Lockwood Scribe.

The Association was opened by prayer & a Sermon from 1st Cor^{ans} ix. 27th preached by the Rev^d M^r. Stone.

The Questions proposed by the General Association for the discussion of the particular Associations were by a majority of the particular Associations determined in the negative.

The Association took into consideration and discussed those questions.

The Association adjourned till half after five o'clock tomorrow Morning.

Met according to adjournment. The Association resumed the discussion of the Questions under consideration the last evening. They were largely debated by the members of the General Association. A large majority gave their Opinion in favor of the negative; but in consideration that a few particular Associations had not discussed the Questions they were referred to further Examination in the particular associations and the result of their enquiries to be laid before this Body for their opinion at their next meeting.

The following Questions were read and *Voted* to be offerred to each particular Association for discussion, and return be made to the General Association at their next meeting, viz:

I.st Did the human Soul of Christ, exist before the Conception of his Body by the Virgin?

II.^{d} What is the evidence from the Scriptures that there are three persons in the Deity eternally distinct from each other?

Voted that Copies of all Addresses, Draughts, &c made by the General Association be left with the Register of General Association.

Voted that this Question be offered to the particular associations for consideration, and that returns be made to the General Association at their next meeting viz: Whether it be expedient that a minister be appointed by the General Association yearly to preach in the first Church in Hartford on the afternoon of the Genl Election day a Sermon in support of some essential Point of Christianity, and that such sermon, written out in fair hand be lodged from year to year with the associational Register, for the purpose of Selection, for future Publication: That the preacher be not appointed by rotation from the several Associations, but from the State at large.

Voted that the Revd Timothy Stone be appointed to preach the Sermon the day after the next Commencement.

Voted that the next General Association be at the House of the Revd Timothy Dwight D.D.

Test W. Lockwood, Scribe.

NOTES.

1. Charles Backus   Pastor in Somers   from 1774 to 1803.
2. William Lockwood   "   Milford   "   1784 " 1796.
3. Joseph Vaill   "   Hadlyme   "   1780 " 1832.
4. John Noyes   "   Weston   "   1786 " 1807.
5. Jason Atwater   "   Branford   "   1784 " 1794.

1790.

At a meeting of the General Association of Connecticut, at the House of the Revd Timothy Dwight D.D. June 15th 1790 —

Present

The Revd Messrs
- Samuel Lockwood D.D.
- Nathaniel Taylor
- Nathaniel Bartlett
- Robert Ross
- Judah Champion
- Elizur Goodrich D.D.
- Ebenezer Kellogg
- Benjamin Trumbull
- John Foot
- Aaron Church (¹.)
- Rufus Hawley (².)
- William Seward
- Timothy Dwight D.D. (³.)
- Nathan Fenn
- Henry Ely
- Zebulon Ely

The Revd Nathaniel Taylor was chosen Moderator, and Mr Benjamin Trumbull was chosen Scribe.

The meeting was opened with prayer offered and a Sermon preached, by the Revd William Seward from Dan. ii: 44.

Voted, That the two questions proposed to the particular Associations by the last General Association, for the present be dismissed.

A motion made by the delegates of the western Association of Fairfield county respecting a general union of the Congregational and Presbyterian churches throughout the United States of America, was taken into serious consideration and largely debated: On which the following question was proposed, Whether in the opinion of this Association, any further degree of union between the churches of this State and their brethren of the Congregational and Presbyterian churches throughout the United States of America would be expedient and desirable? Passed in the affirmative.

Voted also, That in the opinion of this Association, this purpose might be effected in some good measure, by letters of correspondence respecting the state of the churches and of religion in the several States, and the different prevailing sects and the impostors that shall arise from time to time with authentic information of their characters, and such other matters as may be thought conducive to the general promotion of the gospel and the prosperity of the churches.

The following gentlemen, Dr. Goodrich, Mr. Huntington of Middletown, Dr. Dwight and Mr. Eliot were accordingly appointed a committee, to correspond with our brethren of the congregational and presbyterian churches in the United States, to communicate to them this resolve, and to desire their opinion on the best method of accomplishing the valuable ends.

Voted also that it is the opinion of this Association, that if the several Associations shall approve of this correspondence, that it be continued from year to year in such manner as shall hereafter be thought best.

Voted that in future meetings of this Association, immediately after opening a docket shall be made out of whatever matters are to be considered by them.

Whereas this Association sometime since desired Mr. Benjamin Trumbull to write a religious history of the late American revolution, and as he hath expressed his wishes that the Association would appoint a committee to inspect said history and report their opinion concerning it to this body at the next general Association, Voted the Revd Drs Goodrich and Dwight, and John Trumbull Esqr of Hartford be a committee for that purpose; and they are desired to inspect the papers which Mr Trumbull shall lay before them, and report as aforesaid.

Voted That the Reverend Isaac Lewis preach the conscio at the next Commencement.

Voted That the next General Association be at the House of the Reverend Noah Merwin of Washington.

The following persons were returned as candidates in the several Counties viz:

Hartford County

North Association = Mr Ebenezer Kingsbury.

Hartford South Association Messrs
- Weight Cornwall
- Calvin White
- Sylvester Sage
- Gad Newel
- Joseph Camp
- Asahel Hooker
- Silas Churchil
- Isaac Porter

New Haven County

Western District Messrs
- Ebenezer Fitch
- Daniel Crocker
- Reuben Morse
- David H. Williston
- Aaron Woodward

Eastern District Messrs.
- Aaron Cook Collins
- William Stone
- Caleb Johnson
- Isaac Maltby
- Oliver Dudley Cook
- Hezekiah Goodrich

Fairfield County

Eastern District — None.

Western District Messrs { William Brintnal Ripley
Samuel Sturgis

New London County.

No returns from either district

Windham County

Messrs { Stephen Williams
Hendric Dow
Dyar Throop Hinkley
—— —— Woodworth

Litchfield County

M.r Chauncy Lee

County of Middlesex

None returned.

Tolland County

Messrs { Azel Backus
Freegrace Reynolds
—— Hyde

True minutes of the General Association
Test BENJAMIN TRUMBULL Scribe.

NOTES.

[1]. Aaron Church Pastor in E. Hartland from 1773 to 1815.
[2]. Rufus Hawley " W. Avon " 1769 to 1820.
[3]. Timothy Dwight " Greenfield " 1783 to 1795.

1791.

At a meeting of the General Association of the State of Connecticut at the house of the Rev.d M.r Merwin in Washington June 21 : 1791, were

Present

Rev.d Mess.rs
- Nathaniel Bartlett
- Cotton Mather Smith
- John Smalley
- David Brownson (¹.)
- Samuel Camp
- John Foot
- Jonathan Edwards D. D.
- Rufus Hawley
- Elijah Parsons
- Timothy Dwight D. D.
- Noah Merwin
- Samuel Stebbins (².)
- Jason Atwater
- Timothy Langdon (³.)
- William Lyman

Mr. Bartlett was chosen Moderator, and Doct. Edwards, Scribe.

The Association was opened with prayer and a Sermon preached by the Rev.d Cotton Mather Smith from John vii : 17.

An application was made to this Association from the first Church in Litchfield for advice respecting the case of Jedediah Strong Esq., who hath been divorced from his wife and the association gave their advice in a letter, a copy of which is on file.

On the request of the Rev.d M.r Trumbull of North Haven the committee appointed by the last General Association to inspect his history was reappointed to the same business.

Voted that henceforward the General Association shall sit circularly in the several associations in the State, in the following rotation; 1. The Western Association in New Haven County. 2. The Eastern Association in D⁰. 3. The Southern Association in Hartford county. 4. Middlesex Association. 5. New London Association. 6. Windham Association. 7. Tolland Association. 8. The Northern Association in Hartford county. 9. Litchfield Association. 10. The Western Association in Fairfield county. 11. The Eastern Association in D⁰. And that the preacher before the General Association, be annually appointed, by the particular association, within the limits of which, the last preceding session of the General Association, save one, shall have been holden.

The Rev ᵈ Jeremiah Day was appointed to preach the *Concio ad Clerum* at the next Commencement.

Voted that it be referred to the particular Associations, whether there shall be an alteration of the time of the session of the General Association, leaving it to the General Association to fix the time of the session, in case an alteration shall be made.

Upon motion Voted That it be recommended to the several congregational ministers, in this State, and it is hereby recommended to them, to obtain an accurate account of the whole number of persons in their respective parishes; and to note the number belonging to each religious denomination, and to make a written return thereof, to the next General Association. And it is further recommended to the several associations in this State, to carry this vote into effect, as well with respect to vacant parishes as to others.

Resolved, That Doct ʳ Edwards, Doct ʳ Dwight, M ʳ. Trumbull, Doct ʳ Goodrich, Doct ʳ Stiles, M ʳ Hinsdale and M ʳ Hart, or any three of them, be a committee of this association, to meet, at New Haven on the second Wednesday in September next, to confer with a committee of the General Assembly of the Presbyterian church in the United States, concerning some proper mode of future correspondence between the churches of this State, and the said General Assembly, and to report to this association at the next session.

Resolved that there be preached annually in the Brick meeting-house, at New Haven, on the day preceding the commencement, at 4 oclock P. M. a sermon on the *Evidences of the Christian Religion*, and that the preacher leave a fair copy of his Sermon with the Register of this Association, to be disposed of by the direction of the Association; and that the preacher be appointed by this Association annually out of the State at large.

The Revd Mr Smalley was appointed to preach, agreeably to the above resolve, at the next commencement.

The next General Association was appointed to be holden at the house of the Reverend Mr Leavenworth at Waterbury.

Voted that it is hereby recommended to the several Associations to express their views concerning the most proper and feasible mode of sending missionaries to the new settlements, and to communicate them to the next General Association.

Voted also that the subject of the examination of candidates for the ministry in the learned languages, arts and Sciences, and ecclesiastical history, as well as theology, be referred to the consideration of the next General Association.

The following is the list of Candidates returned to this Association.

New Haven County

Western Association
  Ebenezer Fitch
  Reuben Moss
  David H. Williston
  Aaron Woodward
  Dan Bradley
  Giles H. Cowles
  Joel Bradley

Eastern Association.
  William Stone
  Caleb Johnson
  Oliver D. Cook
  Hezekiah Goodrich

Hartford County.

Southern Association
Wait Cornwell
Gad Newell
Joseph Camp
William Fowler Miller
Asael Hooker
Isaac Porter
James Cassen Guernsey
Israel Bard Woodward
Stephen Fenn

Northern Association
Ebenezer Kingsbury.

Fairfield County

Western Association
William Brintnal Ripley
Samuel Sturges

Eastern Association
None.

New London Association
No return.

Windham Association
No return.

Litchfield Association
None.

Tolland Association
No return.

Middlesex Association
John Eliot.

Voted to be true minutes of the proceedings of the General Association.

Test JONATHAN EDWARDS Scribe

NOTES.

'. David Brownson Pastor in Oxford 1764–1806.
². Samuel Stebbins   "   Simsbury 1777–1806.
³. Timothy Langdon   "   Danbury 1786–1801.

1792.

At meeting of the General Association of the State of Connecticut, at the house of the Rev.ᵈ Mark Leavenworth in Waterbury on the third Tuesday of June A.D. 1792. Present Revᵈ Messʳˢ

Judah Champion Simon Waterman	Litchfield County.
Elijah Lothrop Nathan Williams	Tolland County.
Amos Fowler ('.) James Noyes (².)	Eastern District New Haven County.
Mark Leavenworth Jonathan Edwards	Western District New Haven County
Theodore Hinsdale Nathaniel Gaylord (³.)	Hartford North Association.
Cyprian Strong William Robinson (⁴.)	Hartford South Association.
Elijah Parsons Achilles Mansfield	Middlesex County.
Aaron Kinne David Hale (⁵.)	New London County
Zebulon Ely Elijah Gridley (⁶.)	Windham County
Isaac Lewis Matthias Burnet (⁷.) David Ely	Western District Fairfield County
Timothy Langdon	Eastern Association Fairfield County

The Revᵈ Mʳ Leavenworth was chosen Moderator, and Mʳ Strong Scribe.

The Association was opened by prayer, offered by the Rev.ᵈ Mʳ Lathrop. Returns were made from several particular Associations, relative to several things referred to them, by the last General association. Minutes of the proceedings of the Convention of the committees of the Assembly of the

Presbyterian churches in the United States and of the general Association of this State. A Letter from the Rev⁴ Benjamin Trumbull was received and read. Reports from the several particular Associations as to the expediency of altering the time for holding the General association were made. Whereupon the Association Voted, That they would do nothing relative to making an alteration as to the time of holding the General Association.

Attended public worship, When a Sermon was preached by the Rev⁴ Mʳ Lewis from John VII: 17.

The Association entered upon the consideration of the recommendation of the last General Association relative to an enumeration of the inhabitants of parishes &c. From the returns made by the particular Associations it was Voted — Not to prosecute the measure any further.

The most feasible and proper mode of sending missionaries to the new settlements nextly came under consideration: and was referred to a committee to report tomorrow morning.

Mʳ Williams and Doct. Edwards were appointed the Committee.

Adjourned till half after five o'clock tomorrow morning. Met according to adjournment. The association of the County of Middlesex having informed the general association that they had appointed the Rev.⁴ Mʳ. Vaille as a missionary to the new settlements; although the proper season is passed for the other associations to adopt similar measures, yet the General association approved the laudable zeal of the association in Middlesex and recommended Mʳ Vaille to the notice and attention of the inhabitants of the new settlements, as a regular and worthy minister of the gospel.

The committee appointed Yesterday reported a petition to be presented to the General Assembly of this State, praying for a Brief &c. as appears from a copy of sᵈ petition on file. The Rev⁴ Messʳˢ Jonathan Edwards D.D., Ezra Stiles D.D. and Mʳ Nathan Williams were appointed a Committee to prefer the above said petition to the General Assembly; and also a Committee to join a Committee from the Assembly, in case said petition be granted, to receive and pay out such monies as may be collected.

On the Question respecting the examination of Candidates for the Ministry in the Languages, Arts and Sciences as well as Theology, the Association finding, that several of the Associations are already in the practice, consider it as a commendable practice, and wish for uniformity in it — But agree that any diversity of sentiment or practice, on this point, shall not at all interrupt the harmony of our proceedings.

On the request of the Revd Mr Trumbull of North Haven, the committee appointed by the last General Association, to inspect his history was reappointed to the same business.

The following questions from New London Association, were proposed to the General Association Viz:

1. Is it the duty of the Churches to require a Confession from Candidates for admission into Church fellowship, for scandalous sins previously committed?

Answered in the affirmative.

2. Is it expedient that all confessions for public crimes should be made before the Congregation, or is it sufficient that they be made before the Church only?

Answer — Before the Congregation.

The Association then proceeded to consider, and did approve of the doings of the Committees from the Assembly of the Presbyterian churches in the United States, and the General Association of this State: — And Voted That a Committee of three be appointed to attend the next General Assembly of the Presbyterian Churches. — Revd Messrs Matthias Burnet, Jonathan Edwards D. D. and Timothy Dwight D. D. were chosen said committees.

Voted That the former Committee of correspondence be continued for the present year. That the Revd Messrs Nathaniel Taylor, Nathan Williams, Thomas W. Bray, Benjamin Trumbull, Eliphalet Williams D.D., William Robinson, John Devotion, Levi Hart, Timothy Stone, Isaac Lewis and David Ely be a standing committee to certify the good qualifications of such preachers as travel from the limits of the churches in this association into the limits of the presbyterian Churches.

The Revd Theodore Hinsdale was chosen preacher on the evidences of the Christian Religion on the day preceeding the next public commencement at New Haven.

Revd Jonathan Edwards was appointed preacher of the *Conscio ad Clerum*, at the Chapel in New Haven the day after Commencement.

Voted, That it be the duty of the preacher of the Sermon on the evidences of the Christian Religion, on the day preceding the Commencement at New Haven, to convey a copy of said sermon to the Register of the general Association, before the setting of the next general Association, after the delivery of said sermon; and that the Register transmit to the said general Association the copies of such sermons as are lodged with him.

Voted That whereas a division hath taken place in the Association in Litchfield County known by the name of the Northern and Southern Association in Litchfield County, since the order of the Rotation of the general Association was fixed, That the General Association remove from Hartford north to Litchfield north Association, from thence to Litchfield south Association, then in the order stated June 21^{rt} 1891, and that the southern Association in Litchfield county provide a preacher for the next general Association. .

Voted that the next general Association be holden at the house of the Revd Mr Foot in Cheshire.

The following is a list of Candidates returned to this Association.

New Haven County Western District.

Ebenezer Fitch, David H. Williston, Aaron Woodward, Giles Cowles, Joel Bradley, William Brown, and Benjamin Wooster.

New Haven East District

Caleb Johnson, Hezekiah Goodrich.

Hartford South

Gad Newell, Joseph Camp, Isaac Porter, James C. Guernsey, Stephen Fenn, and Asahel S. Norton.

Hartford North

Calvin Chapin.

Fairfield County Western District

Samuel Sturgis.

Eastern District — None

New London — None

Windham

Timothy Williams, Edmund Freeman, Dyer I. Hinkley, —— West, —— Rockwell, —— Spalding, Stephen Williams.

Litchfield — None

Tolland.

Freegrace Reynolds, Uri Tracy, Silas Long Bingham, —— Lyon, John Taylor.

Middlesex — None.

Voted to be the minutes of the proceedings of the General Association.

CYPRIAN STRONG, Scribe.

NOTES.

[1]. Amos Fowler — Pastor in Guilford — 1758–1800.
[2]. James Noyes — " " Wallingford — 1785–1832.
[3]. Nathaniel Gaylord " " W. Hartland — 1782–1823.
[4]. William Robinson " " Southington — 1780–1821.
[5]. David Hale " " Lisbon — 1790–1803.
[6]. Elijah Gridley " " Mansfield — 1789–1796.
[7]. Matthias Burnet " " Norwalk — 1785–1806.

1793.

At a meeting of the General Association of the State of Connecticut at the house of the Revd Mr Foot, Cheshire June 18, 1793.

Present

The Revd Messrs
- Nathaniel Taylor
- John Willard
- Cotton M. Smith
- Elizur Goodrich, D. D.
- Richard Ely
- Nathan Williams
- Noah Benedict
- Benjamin Trumbull
- Ammi R. Robbins
- Isaac Lewis, D. D.
- Aaron Kinne
- John Foot
- Jonathan Edwards D. D.
- Nathan Strong
- David Ely
- Nathan Perkins
- William Robinson
- Benoni Upson
- Stephen Stebbins
- Walter King (¹.)
- Samuel Goodrich (².)
- David Higgins (³.)
- Elijah Gridley (⁴.)
- William Storrs (⁵.)

The Revd Doct. Goodrich was chosen Moderator, and Jonathan Edwards was chosen Scribe.

Mr Perkins and Dr Lewis were appointed to assist the scribe in preparing the Docket of the business proper to be done by this association and to report immediately after opening the association by divine service.

The association was opened with a sermon by the Rev^d M^r. Benedict from II Corinthians IV, 4, 5.

The committee aforesaid reported a docket of the business to come before the Association.

The Revd Doct. Rogers of the Presbytery of New York, the Revd Mr Woodhull of the Presbytery of New Brunswick, and the Revd Mr Woodworth of the Presbytery of Long Island produced proper credentials of their appointment by the General Assembly of the Presbyterian churches in America to represent that body in this association, and took their seats accordingly.

The said delegates from the General Assembly of the presbyterian church, laid before this association some proceedings of the General Assembly on the case of the Rev. A. C. Collins and the consideration of that business was voted to be taken up tomorrow morning at 8 o'clock.

Mr Perkins was appointed assistant Scribe. Doctor Dwight was appointed to preach the Sermon on the Evidence of Christianity on the day preceding the next commencement. Voted that henceforth it be a rule of this association that a second to the preacher on the evidence of Christianity be annually appointed. Doctor Edwards was appointed a second to the preacher on the evidence of Christianity for this year. Adjourned till tomorrow morning 6 o'clock.

June 19th 6 o'clock A. M. met according to adjournment, and adjourned to the meeting house.

Voted That the committee appointed for the inspection of Mr Trumbull's general History of the United States of America be continued, and that it is the desire of this association, if on inspection, they shall esteem it worthy of public notice, they encourage him to exhibit proposals for its publication, with such joint recommendation of theirs, as they shall judge expedient.

On motion from the association of the Western district of New Haven County, the following question was put, Whether a professed belief of the final salvation of all men be a censurable heresy ? which passed in the affirmative.

The Rev⁴ T. W. Bray was appointed to preach the Conscio ad Clerum at the next Commencement.

8 o'clock A. M. the Association took up the order of the day, and the minutes of the General Assembly directing their delegates to lay before this association all the proceedings and documents relating to the case of Mr A. C. Collins were read; and Mr Collins requesting that he might be heard on the propriety of laying those documents before this association, the question was put, Whether the delegates be permitted to lay the said documents before this Association at at this time? And it passed in the affirmative.

After the hearing of the delegates, Mr Collings had full opportunity to say all he wished to say. Then the question was put, Whether this association accept of the reference of the case of Mr Collins to this association? Which passed in the affirmative. Mr Foot, Mr Robbins and Dr Rodgers were appointed a committee to bring in a report of the proper measures to be adopted and pursued in the case of Mr Collins.

On motion from the Windham association respecting measures for the promotion of Religion, as an expedient for this desirable end this association earnestly recommends frequent religious conferences, and a spirit of abundant prayerfulness, and that these conferences be under the immediate inspection of the respective pastors of the churches.

The committee on the case of Mr Collins brought in a report which was not accepted. Then on motion, Voted, That it is expedient that the case of Mr Collins be tried at Salisbury. Also Voted that it shall be tried by a Consociation. 3^{ly} That it be tried and issued by the consociation of the northern district of Litchfield county. 4th That the said consociation is requested to meet at the meeting House in Salisbury for the trial of the case aforesaid on the third Tuesday of August next, and that a letter from this association be sent to the Moderator of the last Consociation in the northern district in Litchfield county communicating the proper information on this subject. The Scribe of this association was directed to furnish Mr Collins and the appellants at Morristown with copies of the votes of this association relative to him, and that this be sufficient notice for their future direction in the case

Voted, That the missionaries to the new settlements shall spend the time of four months in their missions, and that they be allowed four dollars and an half per week, over and above four dollars for the supply of their pulpits during their absence.

Voted, That whatever voluntary contributions shall be received by any of the missionaries, shall be accounted for by them to this association, or the committee appointed by the General Assembly. The missionaries appointed are Messrs David Huntington, Ammi R. Robbins, Samuel J. Mills, Cotton M. Smith, Joseph Vail, Samuel Eells, Theodore Hinsdale, and Moses C. Welsh.

Voted, That president Stiles, Messrs Nathan Williams and Benjamin Trumbull, Doctor Edwards and Mr Thomas Wells Bray be a committee to draw up a plan of the missions and an address to the people of the new Settlements, and to fill up the places of those gentlemen, who may fail of fulfilling the missions to which they are appointed, and if the fund afford it, to appoint new gentlemen on the mission, any three or more of them to act.

On the Motion from Tolland association concerning a fund for ministers widows, Voted, That Messrs Nathan Perkins, Nathaniel Williams, and Nathan Strong be a committee to collect information relative to that subject, and communicate it to the several associations of this State, that they may send their opinions to the next general association.

The committee to draw up a plan of the missions, if they judge it expedient, are desired to publish at some convenient time before the first of May next, an account of the receipts and expenditures of the monies contributed, and a narrative of the missions.

The moderator was requested to return the thanks of this association to the editors of the American preacher, for the twelve Books of the American preacher presented by them to this association, and it was Voted, that the said twelve Books be distributed one to every association.

Mr Taylor, Doctor Lewis, and Mr Perkins were appointed to represent this association in the next General Assembly of the Presbyterian church.

The same committee of correspondence and certification appointed last year, were continued for another year.

Whereas the association of the County of Windham have manifested to this association their desire, that there may be a meeting of each consociation in this State at least once a year, who by their delegates shall form a general consociation of the State, to meet annually; Voted that it be recommended to the several associations to consider of the matter and make report of their opinion to the next general association. The reasons urged for this proposition, are the advancement of union and mutual Christian intercourse, uniformity and energy in the discipline of Christ's church; the promotion of mutual confidence between the clergy and layity, and uniformity in the mode of ecclesiastical processes in the several parts of the State. It is earnestly requested that each association will consider this matter with their usual candor, and whether they adopt or reject, that they will assign their reasons for so doing.

Voted, That the scribe be directed to inform Mr Smalley that this association regret that he has not complied with the vote of the last association in depositing his sermon on the evidence of Christianity with the Register, and expect that he forthwith comply with the said vote.

The following is the List of the present Candidates for the ministry.

New Haven Western destrict.

Ebenezar Fitch, Aaron Woodward, Joel Bradley, Benjamin Wooster, Platt Buffet, Joseph Goff, Edward Dow Griffin.

New London Association

John D. Perkins, Elijah Waterman.

Fairfield West Association

James Richards 3rd.

Windham Association.

Timothy Williams, Dyer L. Hinkley, Lothrop Rockwell, Solomon Spaulding, Stephen Williams, Lynde Huntington.

Litchfield Association.

Nathan Eliot.

Tolland Association

Freegrace Reynolds, Uri Tracy, Silas Long Bingham, and Fields.

New Haven East Association

Caleb Johnson.

Hartford South Association.

Gad Newel, Isaac Porter, Joseph Camp, James C. Guernsey, Stephen Fenn, Asahel S. Norton, Whitefield Cowles, Silas Churchill.

The next General Association was appointed to meet at Mr Upson's in Kensington.

Voted to be true minutes.

Test JONATHAN EDWARDS Scribe.

NOTES.

[1]. Walter King   Pastor 2d Norwich 1778–1811.
[2]. Samuel Goodrich "   Ridgefield 1786–1811.
[3]. David Higgins Missionary to New Settlements.
[4]. Elijah Gridley Pastor, Mansfield 1789–1796.
[5]. William Storrs   "   Westford 1790–1824.

1794.

At a meeting of the General Association of the State of Connecticut at the house of the Rev.ᵈ M.ʳ Upson, Berlin, June 17, 1794.

Present —

The Rev.ᵈ Messrs.
- Nathan Williams
- Simon Waterman
- Levi Hart
- John Marsh (¹.)
- Thomas W. Bray
- Samuel Eells
- Dr. Jonathan Edwards
- Dr. Timothy Dwight
- David Ely
- Alexander Gillet (².)
- Achilles Mansfield
- Nathan Perkins
- David Huntington (³.)
- David Tullar (⁴.)
- Nehemiah Prudden (⁵.)
- Benoni Upson
- Enoch Pond (⁶.)
- Henry Ely
- Zebulon Ely
- Jonathan Miller (⁷.)
- Walter King
- Samuel Goodrich
- Standley Griswold (*.)
- Dr. Alexander McWhorter
- Jedediah Chapman.

These two last gentlemen of the Presbytery of N. York, produced proper credentials of their appointment by the general Assembly of the Presbyterian church in America, to represent that body in this Association, and took their seats accordingly.

The Rev⁴ Nathan Williams was chosen Moderator and D⁻ Jonathan Edwards and Nathan Perkins Scribes. The Association was opened with prayer by the moderator.

The Rev⁴ Levi Hart, John Marsh and Thomas W. Bray were appointed a committee together with the scribes, to prepare the Docket of the business proper to be done by this Association.

The Association voted that it be the duty of the moderator always to open the session of the Association in the morning, and to close it in the evening with prayer; also that whenever the moderator wishes to deliver his sentiments on any subject which shall be in debate before this association, he shall quit the chair, and the scribe shall take it, during the time that the moderator shall be speaking.

Adjourned for public worship, and the sermon was preached by Dʳ Edwards from Phil II: 13.

Met according to adjournment. The Rev⁴ Levi Hart was appointed a second, as preacher on the Evidences of Christianity, at New Haven on the day before the next commencement.

The committee of Correspondence, Dʳ Goodrich, Enoch Huntington, Dʳ Dwight, and Andrew Eliot was continued.

The Rev⁴ Nathan Williams, Thomas W. Bray, Benjamin Trumbull, Dʳ Eliphalet Williams, William Robinson, John Devotion, Levi Hart, Timothy Stone, Dʳ Isaac Lewis, David Ely, Simon Waterman and Ammi R. Robbins were appointed the committee to give certificates of the good character and qualifications of preachers who travel into the bounds of the Presbyterian church.

The proceedings of the several Associations concerning a general Consociation were exhibited, and Mʳ Hart, Dʳ Dwight, Mʳ Bray, Mʳ David Ely, and Mʳ Marsh were appointed a committee to make a draught of a plan of a General Consociation, and to make report tomorrow morning.

Adjourned till tomorrow morning 8 o'clock.

Met according to adjournment.

Voted That henceforward it be a rule of this Association,

that the Roll of the Names of the members be called at the beginning of every session.

Voted that the Committee appointed by the legislature of the State to receive the contributions of the several Ecclesiastical Societies in the State render at every General Association, an account of their receipts and expenditures of the money contributed in the preceding year: and that the same committee for superintending the Missions to the New Settlements be reappointed to the same services to which they were appointed the last year.

The committee appointed by the legislature of the State to receive and disburse the contributions for the support of the missions to the New Settlements, gave in their accounts of the receipts and disbursements of the monies contributed for the last year.

Mr Cyprian Strong was appointed to preach the Conscio at the next Commencement.

The committee to make a draught of a plan of a general Consociation brought in their report, which, with the emendations was as follows —

I. That there be, within each associational district in this State, an annual convention of the ministers and of the Churches by their delegate or delegates; who shall appoint, each two ministers and two delegates, to meet in general convention and shall transact any other business, as to each district convention shall appear expedient.

II. That in every vote, all the members of said General Convention shall have an equal voice.

III. That the general Convention transact the same kinds of business, which are now transacted by the general association; and such other business as shall be referred to them by the district Conventions.

IV. That the place of their first meeting be the city of Hartford, and the time, the Monday preceding the general Election, at 4 o'clock in the afternoon.

V. That s'd General Convention exist seven years from its first meeting, and that if two thirds of the district conventions shall then chuse that its form be altered, or its existence terminated, it shall be so altered or terminated; otherwise it shall continue in its former state.

Voted — that the aforesaid plan of district and general conventions be submitted to the several associations in this State and to the churches of their districts for their consideration and their proceedings thereon be returned to this general association at their next meeting.

Voted that D^r. Goodrich, Dr Dwight and John Trumbull Esqr. be continued as the committee of this association to revise and recommend as they shall judge best the Revd Benjamin Trumbull's proposed history agreeably to former votes of this association.

Voted that four months be the term of the missions to the new settlements; that eight missionaries be employed, and that nine dollars a week be the compensation for their services and the supply of their pulpits. And the Revd Messrs Theodore Hinsdale, Aaron Kinne, Moses C. Welch, Jeremiah Day, Asahel Hooker, Azel Backus, Cyprian Strong, William Lyman were appointed missionaries to the New settlements and the committee to superintend the missions were empowered, if they cannot obtain settled ministers to employ at their discretion Candidates in the missions, at four dollars and an half per week for their service.

A Letter from the Presbytery of New York, containing the sentence of deposition from the holy ministry pronounced on Aaron Cook Collins with a request that it be communicated to the respective associations, was laid before the General Association.

The motion for a widow's fund made last year with the papers thereunto relating, was laid over to the next meeting of the general Association.

The motion of the General Assembly of the Presbyterian church, that the delegates from that Assembly to this association, and the delegates from this association to that assembly be empowered to vote in all questions decided in those bodies respectively, was taken into consideration, and after discussion; the General Association voted a compliance with the said proposal.

A Letter from the Committee of correspondence of the convention of the ministers of Massachusetts was read, and the committee of correspondence of this association, was directed to return an answer.

Mr Perkins a delegate from this association to the general Assembly of the Presbyterian Church, gave an account of the proceedings of that Assembly in their last sessions.

The committee to superintend the missions was directed to make enquiry concerning the money contributed before the war for missions to the New Settlements, said to have been deposited in the hands of Dr Goodrich and others, and to put the same into the fund lately contributed for the same purpose.

Mr Hart, Mr Z. Ely, and Mr. Marsh were directed to make a draught of a Letter of thanks to the governor for the Patronage and countenance which he has given to the charitable design of sending missionaries to the new settlements.

Adjourned 'till tomorrow morning 7 o'clock.

Met according to adjournment.

The committee appointed to make a draught of a Letter of thanks to governor Huntington; made their report, and the letter after being corrected was accepted.

Voted that it is expected by the Association that the committee for superintending the missions, charge all necessary expenses attending their service.

Voted that Mr Benjamin Wooster be paid for his service in the New settlement at the rate of four dollars and an half a week, beginning his wages in his first tour at the time of his beginning his service.

The Revd Nathan Strong, Benjamin Trumbull and Nathan Williams were appointed to represent this association in the next General Assembly of the Presbyterian churches in the United States.

The next General Association was appointed at the house of the Revd Mr Hotchkiss of Saybrook.

The following is the List of the present Candidates for the Gospel Ministry.

New London Association — John D. Perkins, Elijah Waterman, Daniel Hall.

New Haven West Association — Benjamin Wooster, Amos Bassett, Platt Buffet, Joseph Goff, Edward Dorr Griffin, Maltby Gelston.

Fairfield west Association — James Richards, Jonathan L. Pomeroy, Jonathan Bartlet, David Hill.

Windham Association — Stephen Williams, Timothy Williams, Solomon Spalding, Mr Witter, Lynde Huntington.

Tolland Association — Free Grace Reynolds, John L. Skinner, Masfield Steel, Silas Long Bingham, Uri Tracy, Mr Fields.

Hartford South Association — Joseph Camp, James C. Guernsey, Silas Churchill, Mr Pinio, Mr Shepherd, Joseph Washborn, Mr Porter. Litchfield South Association — Nathan Eliot. New Haven east Association — Caleb Johnson.

The Association voted to make the following recommendations to the several Associations, viz, This Association considering the importance of Christianity to mankind, the danger to which youth are at the present time exposed, and the duty incumbent on themselves and their brethren to promote the influence of Religion among youth especially, and generally among those of all ages — do resolve,

I. That it be recommended to the several Associations in this State, to return annually to this body an account of the state of their congregations, of the degree of attention to religion existing in them and of their moral situation in general, in such a manner as they shall judge most conducive to the welfare of Christianity.

II. That it be recommended to the ministers of the several Associations to collect the young people of their respective congregations, for the purpose of giving them stated private instruction in the evidences, doctrines and duties of Christianity, and to consider this so far as it may be conveniently done as an important branch of their ministerial Labours.

III. That the meetings for prayer and religious conference recommended by this body, to the ministers and churches of this State, be renewedly urged upon them; this association being strongly impressed with a sense of the usefulness of such meetings not only by the nature of the subject, but also by the happy consequences which have resulted from them, where they have been statedly holden.

IV. That it be recommended to the several Associations to take as effectual care as may be, that students in Theology be employed in their theological education, a sufficient time, and furnished with sufficient advantages, to enable them, to become well acquainted with the doctrines and evidences of Christianity, to instruct others, and to defend those doctrines and support the authority of the Scriptures against unbelievers.

V. And whereas it cannot be expected, that individuals in this country can generally furnish themselves with a sufficient supply of those books, which contain many kinds of very important information in theology and ecclesiastical history, information highly necessary in itself and not easily obtained without the possession of such books; it is therefore recommended to the several Associations to institute associational, circulating Libraries, to consist especially of the most important books relating to the deistical controversy, and to increase them by yearly contributions to such a size as to answer effectually the important purposes here specified.

VI. That it be recommended to the particular associations yearly to inform this body, of the manner and degree in which they comply with the recommendations of this body to them, and in cases of non compliance to send forward their reasons.

Voted to be true minutes of the proceedings of the General Association —

Test JONATHAN EDWARDS, Scribe.

NOTES.

1. John Marsh — Pastor — Wethersfield — 1774–1816.
2. Alexander Gillett — " Torrington — 1792–1826.
3. David Huntington " Salem — 1775–1796.
4. David Fuller " Milford — 1784–1802.
5. Nehimiah Prudden " Enfield — 1782–1815.
6. Enoch Pond " Ashford — 1789–1807.
7. Jonathan Miller " Burlington — 1783–1831.
8. Standley Griswold " New Milford — 1790–1802.

1795.

At a General Association of the State of Connecticut, at the house of the Revd Achilles Mansfield, Killingworth June 16th : 1795   Present

The Revd Messrs
- Cotton M. Smith
- Josiah Whitney (1.)
- Elizur Goodrich D.D.
- John Devotion (2.)
- Nathan Williams D.D.
- Levi Hart
- Elisha Rexford
- Aaron Church
- Thomas W. Bray
- Jonathan Edwards D.D.
- Andrew Lee (3.)
- Achilles Mansfield
- Matthias Bennet
- William Lockwood
- Nathan Fenn
- Lemuel Tyler (4.)
- Amas Chase (5.)
- Stephen W. Stebbins
- Amos Basset (6.)
- Abel Flint (7.)
- Calvin Chapin (8.)
- Asahel Hooker (9.)
- William W. Tennant D.D.
- Ashbel Green D.D.
- John Gammil.

The last three Gentlemen were delegated to this Association, by the General Assembly of the Presbyterian C[hh].

Doctor Goodrich was chosen Moderator, and Doctor Edwards and M[r] Fenn were chosen Scribes. — The Association was opened with prayer by the Moderator. The Association by vote, requested Doctors Tennant and Green to preach a sermon each; one of them this and the other tomorrow evening, as they shall agree between themselves.

Mess[rs] Bray, Heart and Basset were appointed, with the Scribes, to make out a Docket of the business to be transacted by this Association. — The sermon was preached by Doctor Goodrich from 2 Peter iii: 14.

The report of the several Associations concerning a general convention, to be constituted in this State, according to the recommendation of the general Association & particular conventions in the Associational districts, were made, by which it appeared, that the majority of the Associations think it not expedient, that the said measures be at present adopted.

A motion was made from Windham Association, that a particular place be fixed upon, for the stated meeting of the general Association: and it was referred to the consideration of the particular Associations, who are requested to send their sense on this subject, to the next general Association.

Reports were brought in from the several associations, of their proceedings on the recommendation of the last general Association, concerning preaching on the evidences of christianity — instructing youth — the state of their congregations and associational Libraries; which reports contained many things agreeable to the wishes and recommendation of the general Association: and this Association wish the several particular Associations still to prosecute such measures, relative to those subjects, as their discretion and respective circumstances shall point out.

The question concerning seasons of prayer for the revival of religion, came under consideration; and after some deliberation was for the present deferred; and Dr. Williams, Dr.

Green and Mr. Heart were appointed a committee to bring in a draft on that subject.

The accounts of the Committee to receive and disburse the contributions for the new settlements were exhibited, and Mr Lee, Mr Chapin and Mr Tyler were appointed a committee to inspect them and make report. —— Voted that five missionaries to the new settlements be appointed for the ensuing year; and that Nine Dollars a week for the supply of their pulpits and for their services be paid to settled ministers, who shall go upon this service: and that pay to Candidates be six Dollars a week. —— The Revd Messrs Kinne, A. R. Robbins, Knapp, Hart, and Justin Mitchel were appointed missionaries for this year. —— Dr. Williams, Dr. Dana, Dr. Edwards, Mr. Trumbull & Thomas W. Bray were appointed a committee to draw up a plan of the missions and an address to the people of the new settlements, and to fill up the places of those gentlemen who may fail of fulfilling their missions to which they are appointed: and three or more of them to act.

The Revd Mr Trumbull, sent a Letter of resignation of his office as Register of this Association, which was accepted: and the Association voted, that their thanks be returned by the scribe, for his services as Register of this Association.

The Revd Cyprian Strong was appointed Register of the General Association.

A Letter from his Excellency Governor Huntington in Answer to a Letter from this Association at their last session was received and read with much satisfaction. —— A Letter from the sub-committee of correspondence of the convention of Massachusetts was received and read.

Dr. Green laid before this Association, certain papers, relating to the establishment of a Seminary of learning in the State of Kentucky, and a recommendation of that design, by the General Assembly of the Presbyterian Church. This Association having duly considered the case, hereby declare their full confidence in those representations, and full concurrence with the recommendation of the general Assembly.

Certain communications were received from the committee of the Convention of Ministers of the Commonwealth of Massachusetts; and Dr. Tennant, Mr. Bray, and Mr. Whitney were appointed to make report on those communications.

Voted That the Moderator of this Association at any session, shall remain to be the Moderator, until the subsequent session.

Voted; That the Money contributed before the war and sent by Mr Trumbull, by the hand of Dr. Edwards to this Association, be received by Mr. Bray, at its present value; and that Mr Bray, with the advice of the Committee to superintend the missions be impowered to settle, in the best manner with the heirs of the late Revd Warham Williams, with respect to the Money contributed for missions before the war, and now in the hands of the heirs of said Mr Williams, and the said money be applied by him, to the support of the missionaries sent or to be sent into the new settlements.

The committee formerly appointed to revise M^r. Trumbull's history, was continued.

The committee appointed as above to report on the accounts of the Committee to receive & disburse the contributions for the new settlements, made report, which was accepted by the general Association, and ordered to be recorded by the register.

Messrs Cotton Mather Smith, Wm Lockwood and Nathan Fenn, were appointed delegates to the next General Assembly of the Presbyterian Church.— The same committee to certify the good character of traveling preachers, was reappointed.— Mr Mansfield was appointed to preach the *Conscio ad Clerum* at the next Commencement, Dr. Edwards was appointed to preach the next sermon on the evidences of Christianity and Mr. Hart was appointed the second. Dr. Goodrich, Dr. Lewis and Mr. Burnet were appointed a Committee to look up the papers relative to the Convention formerly holden, between the Churches in Connecticut, and the presbyterian Church; and to lay the same before this association at their next session.

Voted That Mr. Cotton M. Smith be allowed his wages as a missionary, during a week that he was sick on his last mission: and that the committee to superintend missions are impowered to make such compensation as they shall judge reasonable, to missionaries that may be taken sick, or be disabled during their mission.

The motion for widows funds laid over to this meeting, was further laid over to the meeting of the next General Association. The List of Candidates is as followeth,

Western Association of New Haven County.

Benjamin Wooster, Platt Buffet and Maltby Gelston.

Eastern Association of the same County.

Caleb Johnson, Roger Harrison and Timothy M. Cooley.

Association in Windham County.

Stephen Williams, Timothy Williams, Ezra Witter, Solomon Spalding, Amasa Porter, Lynde Huntington, Joseph Russell, Daniel Dow.

Association in Tolland County.

Silas L. Brigham, Marshfield Steel, —— Fields, Seth Williston.

Association in New London County.

John D. Perkins, Daniel Hall.

South Association in Hartford County.

Silas Churchill, Ebenezer Porter, Beza Pinco.

Western District in Fairfield County.

Jonathan Bartlit, —— Hill.

As Dr. Edwards has closed his accounts as receiver and disburser of the money contributed for the missions to the new settlements, and his accounts have been examined and approved by the committee of this Association, therefore, the moderator is requested to give a certificate of this to Dr. Edwards.

The report of the committee concerning seasons of prayer was brought in, debated and finally adopted, and is on file. Voted that the communications from the convention of Massachusetts be committed to the Committee of correspondence, & that they return a proper Answer.

The next general Association was appointed to be at the Rev'd Mr. Strong's at Norwich.

Voted to be true minutes of the General Association.

Test JONATHAN EDWARDS
 NATHAN FENN } Scribes

NOTES.

1. Josiah Whitney — Pastor — Pomfret — 1756–1813.
2. John Devotion   "   Westbrook — 1757–1802.
3. Andrew Lee   "   Hanover   — 1768–1830.
4. Lemuel Tyler   "   Preston   — 1789–1808.
5. Amos Chase   "   Morris   — 1787–1814.
6. Amos Bassett   "   Hebron   — 1794–1824.
7. Abel Flint   "   Hartford 2d — 1791–1824.
8. Calvin Chapin   "   Rocky Hill — 1794–1850.
9. Asahel Hooker   "   Goshen   — 1791–1810.

1796.

At a general Association of the State of Connecticut, at the house of the Revd Mr Strong in Norwich 21st June 1796.

Were Present

The Rev^d
- James Cogswell D. D. (1.)
- Nathan^l. Taylor
- Josiah Whitney
- Nathan Williams D. D.
- Cyprian Strong
- Jonathan Edwards D. D.
- David Ely
- Matthias Burnet
- Joseph Strong
- David Tuller
- Abraham Fowler (2.)
- Samuel Mills (3.)
- Ozias Eells (4.)
- Lemuel Tyler
- Stephen W. Stebbins
- Amos Chase
- James Noyes
- John Willard
- William Lyman
- Henry A. Rowland (5.)
- Publius V. Booge (6.)
- Lynde Huntington (7.)
- Danl Smith (8.)
- John McNight D. D.
- Azel Roe.

The two last gentlemen were delegated to this Association, by the General Assembly of the Presbyterian Church.

Dr. Williams was appointed Moderator — Dr Edwards Scribe.

The Association was opened by prayer, and a Sermon was preached, by the Rev.d Cyprian Strong, from Acts 17 : 11 — Mr. Rowland was chosen assistant Scribe. Messrs Whitney, C. Strong & Fuller, with the Scribes, were appointed a Committee to draw up a docket of the business proper to be done by this Association.

Whereas it was, by the last general Association, referred to the associations of this State, to express their opinion to this general Association, concerning the expediency of having a fixed place of session for the general 'association — And, whereas many of the associations have sent only verbal answers to the question — therefore, resolved, that the same question be again referred, and it is hereby referred to the several associations: and they are requested to return their answers in writing, to the next gen' Association, together with the reasons of their decisions.—— Also resolved, generally, that whenever any matter is referred from the general Association to the particular Associations, unless the result of any Association be returned in writing, it shall not be considered as any result at all.

The Committee of correspondence, viz: D.r Dwight, D.r Goodrich, M.r Huntington and M.r Eliot were reappointed.

M.r Benedict of Plainfield was appointed to preach the *Concio ad Clerum*.

The Committee to certify the good character & standing of travelling preachers, viz: M.r Taylor, D.r N. Williams, M.r Bray, M.r Trumbull, D.r E. Williams, M.r Robinson, M.r. Devotion, M.r Hart, M.r Stone, D.r Lewis, M.r David Ely, were reappointed.

M.r Burnet, M.r Whitney & M.r C. Strong were appointed a Committee to inspect the accounts of those gentlemen who hold the money contributed for the missions to the new settlements.

D.r N. Williams, D.r Dana, D.r Edwards, M.r Trumbull & Mr T. W. Bray were re-appointed a Committee to superintend the missions to the new settlements.

Voted — That the sum remaining of the contributions for the missions to the new settlements be nearly expended this year.

Resolved generally, That this Association think it advisable that settled ministers be sent on the mission.

Resolved: That the delegates from this Association to the General Assembly of the presbyterian C^hh shall always make a written report to the next General Association of the fulfillment of their appointment; and of such things in particular as concern the Churches represented in this Association.

Mr Morgan was appointed to a Mission to the new settlements for four months; And Mr Joel Benedict, Mr Nott, Mr Rexford, M^r. Vaile, Mr Mitchel, M.^r McClure, Mr William Lyman and Mr Prudden, were appointed each to a mission of two months; provided those who are appointed for two months shall consent to compute the time and expense of their journey to the new settlements and not those of their return from thence.

The compensation to the missionaries was voted, as was voted the last year.

Mr Tyler was added to the Committee to superintend the mission to the new settlements.

On motion that the general association would devise some measures to perpetuate the missions to the new settlements, resolved, that as there is now a considerable sum remaining of the late contributions, the proposal be laid over for further consideration to the next general Association.

The proposal of a Widows' fund was laid over to the next general association.

Mr Charles Backus was appointed second to the preacher on the Evidences of Christianity, the day previous to the next commencement.

List of Candidates.

Western Association in New Haven County.
Benjamin Wooster, Maltby Gelston, Abraham Allyn.
Eastern Association in D° Roger Harrison.

Windham Association.

Stephen Williams, Timothy Williams, Ezra Witter, Solomon Spalding, Amasa Porter.

Tolland Association.

Marshfield Steel, Zach. More, Joseph Field, Seth Williston.

New London Association.

John D. Perkins, Daniel Hall, Eliphalet Nott.

Hartford South.

Ebenezer Porter, Beza Pinco.

Western District Fairfield County.

—— Hall.

M.[r] Tuller, M.[r] Stebbins, and M.[r] Hart were appointed delegates to the next general Assembly of the presbyterian Church.

The next general Association was appointed to meet at the House of the Rev.[d] M.[r] Waterman in Windham on the third tuesday of June next.

Voted — That it be recommended to the several Associations to take measures to procure regular bills of Mortality in the several societies and towns of this State; and that these bills be annually sent to the general Association.

Voted That the delegates from the Eastern Association of New Haven County are hereby directed to inform M.[r] Bray, that the association expects, that he do what he can toward procuring the money contributed before the war, and supposed to be in the hands of the heirs of the late Rev.[d] Warham Williams, and make report to the next general Association.

The committee to superintend the missions are directed to publish a further narrative of the missions at furtherest at the close of this year.

D.[r] Goodrich, D.[r] Lewis, & M.[r] Burnet are continued as a

Committee to look up the papers relating to the Convention holden before the war, between the Churches in this State and the presbyterian Church.

Voted to be true minutes of the proceedings of the general association.

Test{ JONATHAN EDWARDS } Scribes.
     HENRY A. ROWLAND

NOTES.

1. James Coggswell — Pastor — Scotland — 1772–1804.
2. Abraham Fowler — " — Naugatuck — 1785–1799.
3. Samuel Mills — " — Chester — 1786–1814.
4. Ozias Eells " Barkhamsted 1784–1813.
5. Henry A. Roland " Windsor 1st — 1790–1835.
6. Publius V. Booge " Winchester — 1791–1800.
7. Lynde Huntington " Brandford — 1795–1804.
8. Daniel Smith " Stamford — 1793–1842.

1797.

At a General Association of the State of Connecticut at the house of the Rev.ᵈ Mʳ Waterman of Windham June 20ᵗʰ 1797

Were Present

Rev.ᵈ Mess.ʳˢ Josiah Whitney,
Nathaniel Williams, D. D.,
John Smalley,
Simon Waterman,
Levi Hart,
Hezekiah Ripley,
Samuel J. Mills,
John Foot,
Jonathan Edwards, D. D.,
Achilles Mansfield,
Nathan Perkins,
Joseph Strong,
David Tuller,
Abraham Fowler,
Fredric Wᵐ Hotchkiss,
Timothy Langdon,
Uriel Gridley, (¹.)
Lynde Huntington,
Daniel Waldo, (².)
Giles H. Cowles, (³.)
Daniel Smith,
Elijah Waterman, (⁴.)
Ichabod L. Skinner, (⁵.)
James F. Armstrong,
Samuel Miller, and
James Richards.

The three last mentioned gentlemen were delegated to this general Association, by the General Assembly of the Presbyterian Church in the United States.

Mr Smalley was appointed Moderator, and Dr Edwards, Scribe. The general Association was opened with prayer by the Moderator. The Revd Messrs Whitney, Williams, Hart and Miller were appointed a Committee to draw up a docket of the business.

The sermon was preached by the Revd Achilles Mansfield, from Psalm CXI verse 10. The Revd Charles Backus was appointed to preach the sermon on the evidences of Christianity, on the day preceeding the next Commencement; and the Revd Nathan Strong was appointed his second.

The Revd Mr Brockway was appointed to preach the next concio ad Clerum.

Mr. Smith was appointed assistant scribe. The subject of the widow's fund was laid over to the next general association.

The committee of correspondence viz: D.r Dwight, D.r Goodrich, M.r Enoch Huntington, and M.r Eliot were reappointed.

The committee to certify the good character and standing of travelling preachers, viz: M.r Taylor, D.r N. Williams, M.r Bray, D.r Trumbull, D.r E. Williams, M.r Robinson, M.r Devotion, M.r Hart, M.r E. Waterman, D.r Lewis, M.r David Ely were reappointed.

M.r Whitney, M.r Hart and M.r Perkins, were appointed a committee, to inspect the accounts of those gentlemen who hold the money contributed for the missions to the new settlements.

Dr N. Williams, Dr Dana, Dr Edwards, Dr Trumbull, and Mr T. W. Bray were reappointed a committee to superintend the Missions to the new settlements.

Messrs Joseph Strong, Cyprian Strong, & Timothy Langdon were appointed delegates, to the General Assembly of the Presbyterian Church to meet in Philadelphia on the third Thursday of May next.

The particular Associations having made their returns on the question, whether the session of the general association should be circular, it appeared, that a majority of said associations were in favor of the present circular mode; and therefore, Voted, That the general Association shall, in future, as heretofore, sit circularly in the several associations.

The next general association was appointed to be holden at Mr Bassetts' in Hebron on the third Tuesday of June A. D. 1798.

Mr Strong, Mr Foot, and Mr E. Waterman were appointed a committee to bring in a report concerning the Bills of mortality.

Drs Goodrich and Lewis and Mr Burnett were continued a committee to look up the papers relating to the convention which was holden before the war.

List of Candidates.

New Haven West Association — Abraham Allyn, John Sherman and Isaac James.

New Haven East D^o — Roger Harrison, & Erastus Ripley.

Windham Association — Stephen Williams, Timothy Williams, Ezra Witter, Solomon Spalding, & Amasa Porter.

New London Association — John D. Perkins, Daniel Hall, & Eliphalet Nott.

Tolland Association — Marshfield Steel, Zach^h More, Joseph Fields.

Western District of Fairfield County — David Hill, Zachariah Lewis and Isaac Lewis.

The missionaries to the new settlements appointed for this year are, Mr Solomon Morgan, David Huntington, Mr P. V. Booge, Mr Alexander Gillet, Mr Simon Waterman, and Mr Jesse Townsend.

The committee appointed to bring in a report, concerning the bills of mortality, brought in the following:

Whereas the general Association holden at Norwich June 21: 1796 — did recommend to the several Associations, to take measures to procure regular bills of mortality in the several Societies and Towns in this State, and these bills be annually sent to the General Association — And as the said recommendation is not found sufficiently explicit Voted, that the proposed bills shall exhibit the number of deaths under one year, from one year to five, from five to ten, and then by *tens* to the greatest age — also the sex of the person and the particular disease, with which they die — said Bills commencing on the first day of January 1799 and annually afterwards.

Mr Tullar brought in a report of his executing his commission as a delegate to the General Assembly of the Presbyterian Church —— Mr Hart was added to the Committee to superintend the missions to the new settlements — The compensation of the missionaries was voted to be the same as last year; yet if the committee to superintend the mission, find it necessary to add any thing to the sum granted for supplying the pulpits of the missionaries they were empowered to do it.

Messrs Hart, Strong and Miller were appointed to draught an address to the several Associations on the subject of a missionary Society.

Voted: That the Moderator of every general Association, if he be present at the meeting of the next General Association, shall continue Moderator, until a new Moderator shall have been appointed: if he shall not be present, the scribe of the former General Association, and if *he* shall not be present the oldest member present shall be Moderator until a new Moderator shall have been appointed.

Voted also That all communications from the General Association to the particular Associations shall be attested by the Scribe — Mr Huntington was appointed a Scribe for this purpose.

Mr Mansfield, Mr Mills, Dr Edwards, & Mr E. Atwater were appointed, to bring in a report concerning Mr Barlow's alteration of Dr Watts' Psalms; and they exhibited the following: Whereas in some of Dr Watts's translation of the Psalms, there are expressions confined to particular places or countries; and whereas Dr Watts did not translate some of David's Psalms, therefore resolved by this General Association, that application be made to President Dwight, that he would alter those passages which are confined as aforesaid: and translate those Psalms which Dr Watts did not translate; and that a committee of this body be appointed to review, both the alteration, and translations, which president Dwight shall make, and to correct or approve the same.

Dr N. Williams, Mr Smalley, and Mr Perkins were appointed a committee to act agreeably to said resolve.

A motion being made that a compensation be made to the committee, to superintend the missions, it was laid over to next year.

The committee appointed to inspect the accounts of the committee to superintend the missions reported, that they had inspected the said accounts and found them correct.

The committee appointed to draught an address to the several associations on the subject of a Missionary Society, brought in one which was accepted & is on file.* And Mr Hart, Mr Joseph Strong and Mr King were appointed a committee to make and publish such extracts and summaries as shall be sufficient to give a general view of the subject.

Drs. Dwight, Dana and Trumbull were appointed a committee of correspondence on the subject of a Missionary Society.

Voted: That the committee of publication be directed to make such extracts and summaries from existing publications as will be sufficient to give a general view of the measures adopted in Great Britain and America, for the spread of the gospel in pagan countries, and publish 2000 Copies of their compilation with the address of this body, and distribute 1700 of them to some member or members of the particular associations in the State; so that each minister may have an equal number at or before the second wednesday in september next, that they may circulate through the associations, and by them be distributed to their congregations, in such manner and proportion as they shall judge proper: and the members of this association engage to pay to the committee their respective proportions of their constituents; by the first day of December next; and the committee are directed to reserve 300 copies for the committee of correspondence with missionary societies, to distribute to the friends of Zion in this country and in Europe.

True Minutes

Test { JONATHAN EDWARDS / DANIEL SMITH } Scribes

---

* No such report was among the papers on file as returned to the Register.

NOTES.

¹. Uriel Gridley — Pastor — Watertown — 1784–1820.
². Daniel Waldo — " — W. Suffield — 1792–1809.
³. Giles H. Cowles — " — Bristol — 1792–1810.
⁴. Elijah Waterman — " — Windham — 1794–1805.
⁵. Ichabod L. Skinner — " — No. Coventry — 1794–1798.

1798.

At a meeting of the general Association of the State of Connecticut on the 19th of June 1798 in Hebron at the House of the Reverend Amos Bassett.

Present

Rev.ᵈ Messieurs Benjamin Trumbull D.D.
Simon Waterman
Levi Hart
John Marsh
Hezekiah Ripley
Peter Starr
John Foot
Andrew Lee
Jonathan Edwards D.D.
Nathan Strong
Nathan Perkins
William Lockwood
Joshua Williams
Samuel Blatchford
Zebulon Ely
Justus Mitchel
David Selden
Samuel Nott
Amos Bassett
David L. Bebee
John Eliot
Joshua Leonard
Joel West

Delegates from the General Assembly of the Presbyterian Church —
> Samuel Blair D.D.
> Nathaniel Irwin
> Joseph Clark.

The Rev⁴ Benjamin Trumble was chosen Moderator and the Rev⁴ Messrs Nathan Perkins and John Marsh were chosen Scribes.

The meeting was opened with prayer by the Rev. Moderator.

The Sermon was preached by the Rev. Samuel Nott from 2 Cor. 4: 5.

The Rev. Messrs Hart, Edwards and Strong were appointed a committee to draw up a Docket of the business.

The communications from the district Associations respecting a Missionary Society were read, and the Rev. Messrs Hart, Edwards, Strong and Irwin were appointed a committee to take into view these communications, and report to the Association.

The Rev. Messrs Ripley and Lockwood were appointed a Committee to examine the accounts of the Committee of Missionary publications.

To prevent impositions on Ministers and Churches respecting those who may come from Europe to these United States under the character of preachers of the gospel — Voted That a Committee be appointed to write to the Committee of Ministers, belonging to the Board in London, known by the title of the Fund, or to any known Board of ministers in Scotland, to request them to give Credentials to all Ministers, whom they can recommend for piety and good character, desirous of coming to this Country: and the Committee request those with whom they correspond, to circulate this as extensively as they may judge meet — Voted That Dr. Timothy Dwight, Dr. James Dana, and Dr. Benjamin Trumbull, together with the Rev. Samuel Blatchford be the Committee for this purpose.

No report being made by the Committee to look up the papers relating to the Convention before the war, Dr. Lewis and Mr. Burnett were continued, and Rev. Andrew Eliot and Hezekiah Ripley were added; and Dr. Blair and Mr. Clark were requested to consult the records of the Synod of New York and Philadelphia respecting said Convention, and to forward to Dr. Lewis of Horsneck anything that may throw light on the subject.

The Committee of Missions refused any compensation, being willing to do the service gratuitously.

Dr. Williams, Dr. Dana, Dr. Edwards, Dr. Trumbull, Levi Hart and Mr. Bray were reappointed a Committee to superintend the missions to the new settlements.

The Committee of Missions reported that of the fund there remained 796 dollars, inclusive of what is now due to the Rev. Andrew Judson, for his late services, to be expended in carrying on the benevolent design of advancing the interest of religion in our new settlements in the borders of the wilderness —

And, the Rev. Mess[rs] Andrew Judson, Amzi Lewis, Seth Williston, Walter King, Zebulon Ely and Amos Bassett were appointed Missionaries for the present year.

The Committee to certify the good character and standing of travelling preachers, viz: Mr. Taylor, Dr. Nathan Williams, Mr. Bray, Dr. Trumbull, Dr. E. Williams, Mr. Robinson, Mr. E. Waterman, Dr. Lewis, Mr. David Ely were reappointed.

The Committee of correspondence with the Massachusetts Convention of Ministers viz: Dr. Dwight, Mr. Enoch Huntington, and Mr. Eliot were reappointed, and Mr. Marsh was added.

The Rev.[d] Mess[rs] Nathan Perkins, Samuel Blatchford, and John Eliot, were appointed delegates to the General Assembly of the Presbyterian Church, to meet at Winchester in Virginia, on the third Thursday of May next.

The Rev[d] Cyprian Strong was appointed to preach on the Evidences of Christianity, the day before Commencement, and the Rev[d] Dr. Trumbull second.

The Rev[d] Royal Tyler was chosen to preach the concio ad clerum.

Voted. That this Association will attempt to form a plan for a Missionary Society — The Rev⁴ Levi Hart, Dr. Edwards, Nathan Strong and Nathaniel Irwin were appointed a Committee to report concerning the formation of a Missionary Society — The report was accepted, and the same Committee was appointed to draught a Constitution of a Missionary Society; and the Constitution after due consideration was adopted and is as follows —

"The General Association of the State of Connecticut, impressed with the obligations on all the friends of Christianity, to propagate a knowledge of its gracious and holy Doctrines; Also encouraged by the late zealous exertions for this End, in sundry christian Bodies, can not but hope, the time is near, in which God will spread his truth thro' the whole Earth.— They also consider it as a thing of great importance, that some charitable assistance be extended to new Christian Settlements, in various parts of the United States. The salvation of these souls is precious. The happiness of the rising generation, and the Order and Stability of civil Government are the most effectually advanced, by the Diffusion of religious and moral sentiments, through the preaching of the gospel. In deep feeling of these truths, having by prayer sought the direction of God, in the fear of his great Name, they have adopted the following Constitution of a Missionary Society.

I. This Society shall be known by the name of the Missionary Society of Connecticut.

II. The General Association of the State of Connecticut shall be the Missionary Society.

III. The General Association shall annually, by Ballot, appoint twelve Trustees, whereof six shall be Clergymen, and six shall be brethren of our Churches, who shall conduct the business of the Society in the manner hereafter described.

IV. The objects of the Society shall be, to christianize the Heathen in North America, and to support and promote Christian Knowledge in the new settlements within the United States: and both shall be pursued as circumstances shall point out: and as the Trustees, under the superintendence of the General Association shall direct.

V. The General Association and the Trustees shall adopt such measures from time to time, for raising of Funds, as they shall judge to be expedient.

VI. The Trustees shall have power to apply the Funds of the Society, according to their Discretion, in all cases in which they shall not be limited, by the General Association, or by the Donors.—— They shall correspond with other Missionary Societies — shall have power to appoint and dismiss Missionaries — to pay them, and generally to transact all business necessary to attain the Ends of the Society: and shall be paid their necessary expenses: but shall receive nothing for their services.

VII. The Trustees shall annually appoint a Secretary, who shall keep a fair account of their proceedings, and a Chairman, who with four other Trustees shall be a Quorum to transact Business; — or, if the stated Chairman shall not be present, any seven of the Trustees shall be a Quorum.

VIII. The Chairman shall have power to call a meeting of the Trustees at his discretion, by Letters left with them, or at the houses of their usual residence; and it shall be his duty to call such meetings, whenever requested by two Trustees, and in case of the death of the Chairman, or of his Absence from the State, any two Trustees are hereby empowered to call a Meeting.

IX. The General Association shall annually appoint a Treasurer, an Auditor of Accounts: and the Treasurer shall exhibit both to the General Association and to the Trustees, the State of the Treasury, whenever he shall be called on for that Purpose.

X. The Trustees shall annually exhibit to the General Association a particular account of the Missionaries employed by them — of the places to which they are sent — of the apparent success of the Missions — of the state of the Funds — of their receipts and expenditures and of whatever, relating to this Institution the General Association shall require.

XI. The Trustees and the officers of this Society shall

enter on their respective offices on the first Wednesday of September annually, and shall continue in office for one year.

XII. The Trustees shall hold their first meeting at the State-House in Hartford, on the first Wednesday in September next, at 11 o'clock A. M., and in every year thereafter, they shall meet at the same time and place unless otherwise ordered by the General Association.

XIII. If on experience it shall be found necessary to alter this Constitution, an alteration may be made, by the General Association at their stated Session; but not without having been drawn up in writing and lying under consideration for one year; nor unless at least two thirds of all the members of the General Association shall adopt the said alteration.

The last mentioned Committee were appointed to draw up a Memorial to the Governor and Council, which was reported and accepted — and is on file.

Voted, That Dr Benjamin Trumbull and the Rev. Nathan Strong, or either of them be a Committee to present the Memorial and Petition of this Association to the Governor and Council.

The Reverend Messrs Lockwood, Clark, Lee and Blatchford were appointed a Committee to draw up and report an address to the Inhabitants of the State of Connecticut. The following address was reported and accepted. See the Files.

Voted That the following Civilians and Clergymen be appointed Trustees of the Missionary Society.

Lieut. Governor Treadwell Esqr.

Honble { Jonathan Brace Esqr.
Heman Swift Esqr.

Roger Newbury Esqr.
John Davenport Esqr.
Joshua Lathrop.
Dr. Trumbull
Dr. Edwards

Rev. Messrs { Levi Hart
Nathan Strong
Charles Backus

Cyprian Strong

Andrew Kingsbury Esqr. was appointed Treasurer and John Porter Esqr. Auditor of the Missionary Society.

Voted That the Constitution of the Missionary Society, the address and the Subscription papers be printed to the number of 500 copies; — and the Revd Nathan Strong was chosen to take the Charge of the printing of the same and that the expense of printing be paid by the Committee of Missions.

In Session of the General Association, the subject of means to defray the expense of our Delegates to the General Assembly of the presbyterian Churches, being under consideration, Resolved that the following persons, Lieut. Governor Treadwell, Hon. Jonath. Brace, Revd Nathan Strong, and Nathan Perkins be a Committee to devise and report means to our next Session, adequate to the support of the delegates, which is so necessary for union and interests of the Churches.

Resolved That the Revd Seth Williston be desired, to make as full a Statement as he is able, of the deficiences of support while laboring as a Missionary in the Western settlements since June 1st 1797, to the Committee of Missions; and that the Committee reward him as they reward other missionaries.

Voted that the Revd Messrs. James Dana, Nathan Williams and Thomas Wells Bray, submit all their accounts of the monies lately contributed for Missions to the New settlements to be audited and settled by John Porter Esqr. Auditor of accounts of the Missionary Society of Connecticut; and that they pay over the balances which are in their hands into the hands of Andrew Kingsbury Esqr., Treasurer of said Society, on the first Wednesday of September next.

Resolved by the General Association, That the several associations in this State consider the following Question — Whether Deacons in our Churches ought to be ordained by prayer & imposition of hands: and that they send their decision of the question to the next general association with their reasons.

Voted, That the next General Association in June 3^d

Tuesday 1799 be holden at Hartford at the House of the Rev.^d. Nathan Strong.

Passed in General Association.

Test NATHAN PERKINS, Scribe.

NOTES.

1. Samuel Blatchford — Pastor — Bridgeport — 1797–1804.
2. David Selden — " Middle Haddam — 1785–1825.
3. David D. Beebe — " Woodbridge — 1791–1800.
4. Joshua Leonard " Ellington — 1791–1798.
5. Joel West " East Hampton — 1792–1825.

1799.

At a meeting of the General Association of the State of Connecticut, holden at Hartford the 3^d Tuesday in June 1799 —

The following Gentlemen were present having Certificates of delegation from their several district Associations.

Toland — Nathan Williams D. D. and Charles Backus.
Hartford N — Nehemiah Prudden & William F. Miller.
Hartford S — John Smalley — William Robinson.
Windham C^y — Thomas Brockway, M. C. Welch
Fairfield E — Saml Blatchford — John Ely
Fairfield W — Justus Mitchel — Andrew Elliot.
Middlesex — E. Parsons — L. Rockwell.
Litchfield N — Jonathan Edwards D. D. Saml J. Mills
Litchfield S — Simon Waterman.
New London — Joseph Strong — Levi Hart.
N. Haven — Simon Backus — John Elliot.
N. Haven W — David Tuller — Bazalell Pineo.
From the } John Rogers D. D.
Genl Assembly } Robert Finley.

The Revd Levi Hart was chosen Moderator.
    Samuel Blatchford, Scribe
    John Elliot Assist.^t Scribe

Committee appointed to prepare the Docket { Jonathan Edwards D.D.
John Smalley
Simon Waterman
Robert Finley

The Association was opened by Prayer by the Moderator.

Article 1st

The Report of the Committee appointed to present a Petition to the Governor and Council, to obtain contributions for the support of Missions among the new settlements and the Heathen — Resolved that the Revd Nathan Strong be prepared to present a written report on the subject tomorrow morning.

Article 2.

The Report of the Trustees of the missionary Society — Receipts & expenditures — missions — State of the Fund — Correspondence &c.

A motion was made by the Rev^d Dr. Edwards for the appropriation of one half of the funds on hand for the express purpose of evangelizing the Heathen. After consultation on this motion the Association adjourned at 5 o'clock for divine service — the hour of meeting was appointed at 7 o'clock tomorrow morning — A prayer by the Moderator, concluded the associational business of the day.

In the evening a Sermon was delivered by the Revd Moses C. Welch from Mark 16 : 20.

Wednesday June 19th Prayer by the Moderator. Met according to appointment — The subject of Dr. Edwards's motion was resumed.

Voted by the Missionary Society of Connecticut that one half the monies contributed for the support of missions on the first sabbath in May last, if one half of the monies be yet unappropriated, by the Trustees of the missionary society, or if more than one half of those monies be already appropriated by the trustees, that, then, the whole of those monies now unappropriated ought to be applied by the Trustees to the support of missionaries among the heathen.

In conformity to the Resolve passed yesterday, the Rev.ᵈ Nathan Strong presented a report of the measures taken by the Committee to obtain an act for contributions toward the support of Missions. No 1.

Report of the delegates to the General Assembly.

The delegates appointed by the General Association were unable from various causes to attend — in consequence of which at the request of the Association the Rev.ᵈ Mr. Finley gave an interesting account of the doings of the General Assembly, at their session, together with the most pleasing intelligence received by said Body of the success of the gospel, in several places, and the outpouring of the Divine Spirit.

By a Ballot for the Trustees of the Missionary Society, for the ensueing year, the following Gentlemen were chosen.

The Hon. John Treadwell Esqr.	Rev.ᵈ Benjamin Trumbull
Hon. Heman Swift Esq.ʳ	Rev.ᵈ Nathan Strong
Hon. Roger Newberry Esq.ʳ	Rev.ᵈ Cyprian Strong
Hon. Jonathan Brace Esq.ʳ	Rev.ᵈ Charles Backus
Hon. John Davenport Esq.ʳ	Rev.ᵈ Levi Hart
Doct.ʳ Joshua Lathrop.	Rev.ᵈ Nathan Williams D.D.

By a Ballot for a Treasurer and an Auditor of the accounts of the Missionary Society were chosen

Andrew Kingsbury Esqʳ. Treasurer

John Porter Esqʳ. Auditor of accounts —

A claim of compensation for missionary services being made by the Rev.ᵈ Moses C. Welch, on the part of the Rev.ᵈ Andrew Judson —— the Rev.ᵈ Mess.ʳˢ Andrew Elliot & E. Parsons were appointed a Committee to confer with Mr. Welch and bring in a report on the Subject.

On motion, Voted, that the members of the present Association, do nominate a member in each of their respective associations to be a Committee of Certification ——

The following gentlemen were chosen.

Rev. Dr Lewis Western district of Fairfield County
David Ely Eastern   do.
Dr. Trumbull New Haven West
Mr. Eells —— —— —— East

John Devotion, Middlesex
Joseph Strong, New London
Moses C. Welch, Windham
Dr. Williams, Tolland
Nathan Perkins, Hartford North
William Robinson, —— South
Samuel G. Mills, Litchfield North
Dan Huntington, —— South

Means to defray the expenses of the delegates to the General Assembly —— Voted, that a Committee be appointed to bring in a report on the subject — viz: Rev. Charles Backus, Dr. Edwards, Mr. Smalley.

Several papers relative to the missionary society and business were read.

Dr. Edwards, at his request, was discharged from the Committee of ways and means for the support of delegates & Dr. N. Williams was substituted in his room.

The Committee for the alteration of the Psalm Book made report, which gave rise to a lengthy discussion.

The Committee of ways and means for the defraying of the expenses of the delegates to the General Assembly of the Presbyterian Church reported in the following words —— "The General Association being deeply impressed with the importance of maintaining a free intercourse with the presbyterian Churches in the U. S., and the difficulties which attend a representation in the General Assembly, while our members are left to defray the expenses of their journey, which is frequently the length of several hundred miles; Resolved, That it be recommended to the Several Associations in this State, to lay an annual tax of fifty cents, on each of their members, to be paid to a receiver to be appointed in each Association, and by said receivers to the Treasurer to be annually appointed by the General Association; said sum to be paid by the third Tuesday of June; and the Treasurer is to render an account annually, to the General Association, of his receipts and disbursements. —— The General Association also conceive it expedient, that the compensation allowed to each of the three delegates be fixed at eight cents p.r Mile.

on motion the above report was accepted. The Committee in the case of Mr. Judson made report No. 2.——on which it was resolved, that the General Association find there is due to the Rev. Andrew Judson, the sum of eighty eight Dollars, for missionary services, performed previous to the formation of the missionary society.

On motion Voted, That the following proposed amendment, in the Constitution of the missionary Society of the State of Connecticut, do lie on the table for consideration—That for the words " Who with four of the Trustees shall be a quorum " in Article 7th of the Constitution be substituted the words, " who with five of the Trustees, shall be a quorum."

Bills of mortality were presented from several associations.

On motion adjourned at ½ past 6 o'clock P. M. to ½ past 7 tomorrow morning. Concluded with prayer.

June 20th The Association met according to adjournment — Began with prayer.— On motion Voted, That the Trustees of the missionary society be requested to pay the sum of eighty eight Dollars to the Rev. Andrew Judson, found due to him, according to a previous vote of this Body.

The following Gentlemen were appointed delegates to the next General Assembly of the presbyterian Church. The Rev.d Nathan Perkins, Dr. Lewis, Dr. Edwards.

The subject of Dr. Dwight's alterations of and additions to Dr. Watts' version of the Psalms was resumed — on motion Voted, That whereas a Committee appointed by the General Association, two years since to apply to Doctor Dwight, to alter Dr. Watts' version of the Psalms, have reported, that Dr. Dwight has made alterations &c — Therefore Voted, That this Association examine the alterations, and additions made by Dr. Dwight.

The general Association proceeded to examine the alterations and additions to Dr. Watts' version of the Psalms of David, made by the Revd. Dr. Dwight, and finding it inconvenient to finish the business in their collective capacity,

Voted, That it be committed to a Committee, consisting of four Ministers appointed by this Body, to be joined by a committee, composed of an equal number, to be appointed by the General Assembly of the Presbyterian Church of the U. S., which joint committee shall be empowered to complete the examination, and to recommend it, if they think proper, to the general use of the churches.—— Voted, also, That if the General Assembly shall appoint a committee for the above purpose, that this joint committee shall meet at Stamford on the second Tuesday of June in the year 1800 at 3 o'clock P. M. a majority of which shall be a quorum.

By a ballot were chosen, the Rev.[d] John Smalley, Dr. Lewis, Cyprian Strong & Joseph Strong to be a Committee on the part of the General Association, in compliance with the preceding vote.

The opinions of the several associations, on the question referred to them, for their consideration — " Whether it be duty to ordain Deacons by prayer and Imposition of hands " were called for; and it appearing, that several associations had not sent forward written answers to the above question, a decision on this subject was postponed, and the several associations who are deficient, were desired to send their opinions in writing, with their reasons to the next General Association and the Register is desired to send the returns now made from several associations to the next General Association.

Voted, That the Rev. Nathan Perkins be appointed to preach the *Concio ad Clerum.* Voted, That the Rev[d] Moses C. Welch be appointed the second preacher, on the evidences of Christianity, the evening preceding the next Commencement at N. Haven.

Contributions in the New Settlements &c. Voted, That the Missionaries to the frontiers be instructed, prudently to encourage contributions from the various places through which they itinerate, to aid the missionary funds: and that they account with the Trustees of the missionary Society, for the annual amount of such contributions.

The Committee appointed by the last General Association to correspond with ministers in London, members of the board of Trust, called the Fund, that a determinate method of recommending persons coming from G. Britain whose standing as Ministers is good, be fixed, Reported, that no Letters had been received, in answer to those written to London on the above subject.

Voted; That the same Gentlemen be continued a committee of Correspondence, viz: Rev^d Dr. Benjamin Trumbull, Rev^d Dr. Dwight, and Revd Samuel Blatchford.

On motion adjourned at ½ past 9 o'clock until 5 o'clock tomorrow morning. June 21.

Met according to adjournment — Began with prayer.

A Committee consisting of three members were chosen to correspond with the General Convention of the State of Vermont, and to propose a plan of Union between that Body and the General Association. The Committee chosen were the Revd Messrs Levi Hart and Joseph Strong.

Voted, That the vote of a former Association respecting Bills of mortality be rescinded.

Voted, That the former Committee of Correspondence, with the Massachusetts Convention be continued.

Voted, That the Revd Messrs Cyprian Strong, Charles Backus and Nathan Strong be a Committee to draw up additional Rules, for the regulation of the business of the Genl Association; and that they report to the next session of the G. Association.

List of Candidates.

	Marsfield Steel — Bolton
	Robert Porter — Farmington
	Salmon King — N. Hartford
Tolland	Sylvester Dana — Wilksbury, Pennsylvania
County	Henry Davis — East Hampton, L. Island
	Josiah B. Andrews — Southington
	Vinson Goold — Sharon
	Amasa Jerom — Stockbridge Massa.^{ts}

Western district in N. Haven	Asa Meach — Preston Isaac Jones Jr. — N. Haven Lyman Beecher — N. Haven John Niles — Colchester
Windham	Stephen Williams — Woodstock Timothy Williams — D⁰ Asa Lyman — Lebanon
N. Haven East	Timothy Field — Guilford
Litchfield	———— Gillet Thomas Robbins — Norfolk.

Voted, That the next meeting of the General Association be holden at the house of the Rev. Ammi R. Robbins, at Norfolk on the third tuesday in June.

Voted: That the Rev.ᵈ Abel Flint be Treasurer of the General Association.

Voted: That the following Gentlemen be receivers of the monies to be collected from the particular Associations.

Tolland — Rev. Dr. Nathan Williams
Hartford N. — Nathan Strong
———— S. — William Robinson
N. Haven E. — Matthʷ Noyes
N. ———— W. — Bazaleel Pineo
Litchfield N. — Samuel J. Mills
———— S. — Backus
N. London — Samuel Nott
Middlesex — Elijah Parsons
Fairfield E — S. Blatchford
———— W — Hezekiah Ripley
Concluded with Prayer.

                                       LEVI HART, Moderator.

SAMUEL BLATCHFORD, Scribe.

The following is the copy of Minutes found by Brother David D. Field, and by him left with the Register, suggesting a seeming expediency of their entry, somewhere, among the records of Connecticut General Association, viz.:

At a convention of the committees of the General Assembly of the Presbyterian church in the United States of America, & the General Association of the State of Connecticut, on Wednesday, the 11th of September, 1791, in the Chapel of Yale College: Present—

Rev. Messrs John Witherspoon D.D., Alexander McWhorter D. D. & Jedidiah Chapman, members of the committee from the General Assembly: &

Rev. Messrs Elizur Goodrich D.D., Benjamin Trumbull, Levi Hart, Jonathan Edwards D.D., Timothy Dwight D.D., members of the committee from the General Association.

The convention was opened with prayer by Dr. Witherspoon.

Dr. Rogers was chosen Chairman, & Dr. Dwight Scribe. Dr. Rogers not being in the house, Dr. McWhorter was requested to take the chair.

After conversing, sometime, on the business of the meeting, the convention was adjourned until tomorrow at three o'clock P. M.— prayer being made by Dr. McWhorter.

Thursday 3 o'clock P.M., the convention met, according to adjournment. Dr. Rogers & Mr. Tennant were present & the meeting was opened with prayer by Dr. Rogers.

An extract from the minutes of the convention of the Massachusetts congregational Ministers, May 26, 1791, was read & is as follows viz:

In convention of the Massachusetts congregational Ministers May 26th 1791, an address, signed Elizur Goodrich & Enoch Huntington, respecting a general union of the congregational & presbyterian churches, throughout the United States of America, proposed by the General Association of the State of Connecticut, was read: Whereupon, Voted. That the Rev. Dr. Willard, the Rev. Dr. Howard, the Rev. Mr. Haven, the Rev. Mr. Belknap, & the Rev. Mr. Bradford, be a committee of correspondence on the subject.

Attest JOHN CLARK, Scribe.

Dr. Stiles joined the convention ——— After deliberating on the objects of the meeting, a committee, consisting of Dr. McWhorter, Mr. Chapman, Mr. Trumbull, Mr. Hart and the Scribe, was appointed to prepare a draught, & report it, tomorrow morning.

The convention was then adjourned until tomorrow morning, at nine o'clock, then to meet in the chapel, & concluded with prayer.

Friday morning, 9 o'clock, the convention met according to adjournment, & the meeting was opened with prayer.

The committee appointed yesterday, brought in their report; which being read, considered, amended, & approved is as follows, viz:

Considering the importance of union & harmony in the christian Church, & the duty incumbent on all its pastors & ministers to assist each other, in promoting, as far as possible, the general interests of the Redeemers kingdom; & considering, further, that divine providence appears to be now opening the door for pursuing these invaluable objects, with a happy prospect of success:

This convention are of opinion, that it will be conducive to these important ends, that a standing committee of correspondence be appointed, in each Body, whose duty it shall be, by frequent Letters, to communicate to each other, whatever may be mutually useful to the churches, under their care, & to general interests of the Redeemers kingdom;

That each Body should from time to time appoint a committee consisting of * — (Here is a blank in the original Minutes, to which the following note in the margin, seems directly appended, viz: The blank marked with an asterisk, was, through a mistake, not filled up; & the convention was dissolved, before this mistake was discovered. But six of the gentlemen of the convention, viz: 3 of each committee, unanimously gave their opinion, that it would be most advantageously filled up by the word *Three*) who shall have right to sit in the other's general meeting, — make such communications as shall be directed by their respective con-

stituents — & deliberate on such matters as shall come before
the Body; but shall have no right to vote: that effectual
measures be mutually taken to prevent injuries to the
respective churches from irregular & unauthorized preachers;
to promote this end, the convention judge it expedient, that
every preacher, travelling from the limits of one of these
churches into those of the other; shall be furnished with
recent testimonials of his regular standing, & good character
as a preacher, signed by the Moderator of the Presbytery, or
of the Association, in which he received his license, or, if a
Minister, of his good standing & character, as such, from the
Moderator of the Presbytery, or Association, where he last
resided; & that he shall — previously to his travelling, as a
preacher, into distant parts, further receive a recommendation from one member, at least, of a standing committee to
be hereafter appointed by each Body, certifying his good
qualifications, as a preacher: also that the names of this
standing committee shall be mutually communicated: &,
also, that every travelling, & recommended, as above, &
submitting to the stated rules of the respective churches,
shall be received as authorized preachers of the gospel, &
cheerfully taken under the patronage of the Presbytery, or
Association, within whose limits he shall find employment,
as a preacher: & that the proceedings of the respective
Bodies, on this report, be communicated to our Brethren of
the congregational & presbyterian churches, throughout these
States. . . . . .

The convention then — being concluded with prayer, by
the chairman was dissolved. . . . . . The above are true
Minutes of the proceedings of the convention.

     Attest JOHN ROGERS, } Chairman of the Convention
    TIMOTHY DWIGHT Scribe.

The original paper — handed in by Brother Field — is in
the package of Gen. Assoc^l files, for 1815 — meeting at
Danbury.

INDEX TO SUBJECTS.

Address to the king, 19.
  of condolence, 45.
  to his Majesty and the Princess, 26.
  to the people, 103.
Arminianism, to be protested against, 33.
American Preacher, to be distributed, 149.
Association, General, its organization, 5.
  means for usefulness, 29.
  importance of its doings, 10.
  choice of members, 28.
  time of meeting, 110, 112, 113, 137, 141.
  failure of meeting, 24.
  records of, fail, 40.
  order of sessions, 137, 143.
  duty of Moderator, 152.
  place of meeting, 159, 165, 170.

Baptism, infant, neglected, 91.
  of slaves approved, 6.
Bills of mortality, 167, 171.
Book of discipline to be circulated, 21, 23.

Catechism for children, 23, 42.
Candidates for ministry, examination, 6, 8, 34, 100, 142.
Candidates, discouragements of, 102.
  lists of, 102, 111, 120, 123, 127, 134, 138, 143, 149, 156, 162, 166, 171, 187.
Charge at ordination, how given, 60.
Children, early training of, 23.
  subjects of discipline, 83.
Census of parishes, 137, 141.
Churches, care for vacant, 114, 116.
  disorders in, 14.
  rights of consociated, 44.
  discipline of, 71, 74, 75, 81–4.

Councils, how to call, 8.
  who may sit in, 113.
  consociations the only, 41.
Constitution of Miss. Society, 177–9.
  ecclesiastical, 27, 39.
Consociation, local and general, 27, 28, 30, 31, 41, 149.
  general, shall there be? 149, 152, 153.
  of New Haven County, 34, 43.
  dissatisfaction with, 53, 55.
  causes not appealable from, 72.
Concio ad Clerum instituted, 27, 123.
Communion, terms of, 16, 48.
Complaints, how made, 20.
Confession of faith, new issue of, 36.
  for scandalous sins, 142.
Committees, church, duties of, 83.
  certifying, 142, 152, 183.
Convention, Federal, no God, 126, 129.
  general, of committees, 189.
Contributions for missions, 76, 141, 186.

Deacons, ordination of, 180, 186.
Delegates to General Assembly, 184.
Divorce, when proper, 121, 123, 126.
  of J. Strong, 136.
Divinity, professor of at Yale, 35.
Dissatisfaction with Consociation, how met, 52–3.
Disunion, tendencies to, 106.
Disaffected members not to be encouraged, 15, 21.
Discipline as related to revivals, 14, 18.
  to be enforced, 83, 94, 106.
  questions respecting, 71, 74.
Doctrines as related to revivals, 9, 13.

INDEX TO SUBJECTS.

Elders, to be circumspect and prayerful, 12.
Errors to be avoided, 12, 33.
Episcopacy, its assault repelled, 63.
    petitions for opposed, 71.
Expenses of delegates to convention, 180, 184.

Fasting and prayer recommended, 66, 105.
Family discipline and culture, 82, 104.
Fund for widows, 148, 154, 170.

History of American Revolution, 118, 120, 121, 133, 146, 154.
Husband, rights of, 53.

Indian Academy, support of, 65.
Instructions to delegates, 71.
Immoralities of youth, 100.

Laws, civil, to be enforced, 93.
Letters of dismission, 18.
Letter respecting Wallingford brethren, 41, 42.
    of New York synod, 57.
    to Boston ministers, 77.
    to Governor Huntington, 155, 160.
Licenses, time to run, 113.
    import and authority, 37.
    by whom signed, 41.
Lecture at Commencement, Yale, 118.
Libraries, Associational, 157.
Lord's Supper, when administered, 20.

Masters, duty of, to infant slaves, 6.
Marriage without bans, 118.
Memorial to General Association on divorces, and slave trade, 139.
Meetings for prayer and conference, 157.
Ministers, disorderly, 16.
    duty of discipline, 82.
    rights and injuries of, 72.
    dismissed against their will, 72.
    rights by civil law, 110.
    measures for support of, 55.
    from Europe, 175, 187.

Ministry, importance of a settled, 114.
Minors, may they vote? 16.
Missions, moneys for, 100, 120, 141, 153, 155, 161, 166, 176, 182.
Missionaries to be ordained ministers, 86.
    time and pay of, 148, 154.
    to be sent to new settlements, 79, 81, 85.
    mode of appointment, 107, 141.
    appointments, 80, 160, 166, 171.
    directions to, 80.
Missionary Society, 173, 177.
    treasurer of, 183.
    trustees of, 183.
    quorum of, 185.
Moderator General Association, term of office, 161, 172.

Nonconformity, reasons for, 97.

Ordination of Mr. Day, 118.
    of Mr. Dana, 43.
Ordinances as related to revivals, 14.

Pelagianism to be opposed, 33.
Prayer, special, 38, 66, 159, 163.
    duty and privilege of, 108, 109.
    family, neglect of, 47, 97.
Profanity, prevalence of, 23.
Preachers, Separatist, 113.
    traveling, 170.
Preaching before license, 118.
Printing letter of Non-Conformists, 97.
    Dr. Doddridge's address, 98.
    Dr. Edwards' sermons, 100.

Questions from Rev. Sherman, 72.
    proposed, 121, 131.
    deferred, 123, 131.

Raptures to be avoided, 12.
Records to be distributed, 6.
Reports, annual from associations, 156, 159.
Revival of 1740, 9.
    hindrances to, 13, 14.
Religion, things adverse to, 13.
    decay of, deplored, 66, 105.

INDEX TO SUBJECTS. 195

Reply to letter of synod, 59, 60.
Register, standing, 78.
   resignation and appointment, 160.
Revolution, American, pre-intimated, 77, 86–7.
   address to the churches, 89–96.
   history of, 119, 120, 121.

Sabbath, neglect of, 127.
Scandals deplored, 68.
Sermons, election, 131.
   on evidences, 138, 143, 146.
Separatists, questions about, 113.
   not to be tolerated, 16.
   ordination of, 114.
Slaves, infant, to be baptized, 6.
Slave Trade unjust, 126, 127, 129.
Socinianism to be protested against, 33.
Students to be thoroughly instructed, 157.
Seminary in Kentucky, 160.

Trustees of Missionary Society, 179, 180.

Universalism, is it heresy? 146.
Union of Presbyterian and Congregational churches, 59, 60, 127, 133.

Vice, prevalence of, 23.
   before and during Am. Rev., 86–96.
Voting by defendant, 20.
   manner of in council, 37.
   in convention, 64.

Watts' psalms, alteration of, 172, 185.
Wallingford church troubles, 44, 48, 51.
Wife, rights and duties of, 53.
Wickedness abounding, 92, 105.
Widows, fund for, 148, 154, 170.
Worship, neglect of, 21, 127.

Yale College, professor of divinity, 35.
Youth of the churches appealed to, 95.
   to be instructed, 156.

INDEX OF NAMES.

Adams, Eliphalet, 11.
Atwater, Jason, 132.
Avery, Ephraim, 17.
Avery, John, 119.

Baldwin, Ebenezer, 78.
Backus, Charles, 132.
Backus, Simon, 15.
Bartlett, Nathaniel, 36.
Bartlett, Moses, 22.
Bartholomew, Andrew, 31.
Bassett, Amos, 163.
Beckwith, George, 9.
Beebe, James, 30.
Beebe, David D., 181.
Bellamy, Joseph, 9.
Beldin, Joshua, 45.
Benedict, Noah, 52.
Benedict, Abner, 99.
Bissell, Hezekiah, 22.
Birdsey, Nathan, 22.
Blatchford, Samuel, 181.
Bliss, John, 104.
Bostwick, Ephraim, 7.
Bordwell, Joel, 62.
Boardman, Benjamin, 74
Booge, Ebenezer, 52.
Booge, Publius V., 168.
Brunson, David, 69.
Brinsmaid, Daniel, 73.
Bray, Thomas W., 104.
Brockway, Thomas, 101.
Brownson, David, 139.
Buckingham, Daniel, 30
Burnham, Wm., 5.
Burnet, Matthias, 144.

Cabott, Marston, 19.

Canfield, Thomas, 84.
Camp, Samuel, 124.
Chauncey, Nathaniel, 15.
Chalker, Isaac, 21.
Champion, Judah, 48.
Church, Aaron, 135.
Chase, Amos, 163
Chapin, Calvin, 163.
Clap, Thomas, 5.
Cook, Samuel, 5.
Colton, Benjamin, 11.
Collins, Timothy, 13.
Coggswell, James, 21, 168.
Colton, George, 119.
Cook, Roswell, 129,
Collins, A. C., case of, 146-7, 154.
Cowles, Giles H., 174.

Day, Jeremiah, 109.
Dana, James, trial of, 48, 51.
Devotion, Ebenezer, 15.
Devotion, John, 52.
Dickinson, Moses, 13.
Dorr, Edward, 26.
Dorrance, Samuel, 11.
Drummond, William, 74.
Dunning, Benjamin, 52.
Dwight, Timothy, 135.

Easterbrook, Hobart, 36.
Edwards, Timothy, 7.
Edwards, Jonathan, 122.
Eells, Edward, 28.
Eells, Samuel, 109.
Eelles, Nathaniel, 33.
Eells, Ozias, 168.
Eliot, Jared, 15.
Eliot, Jacob, 17.

INDEX OF NAMES.

Eliot, Andrew, 99.
Ellis, John, 48.
Ely, David, 104.
Ely, Richard, 112.
Ely, Henry, 117.
Ely, Zebulon, 129.

Fenn, Nathan, 122.
Fowler, Amos, 144.
Fowler, Joseph, 30.
Fowler, Abraham, 168.
Foot, John, 74.
Fish, Joseph, 28.
Fuller, David, 158.
Fuller, Daniel, 26.
Flint, Abel, 163.

Gaylord, Nathaniel, 144.
Gaylord, William, 7.
Gold, Hezekiah, 99.
Goodsell, John, 15.
Goodrich, Elizur, 61.
Goodrich, Samuel, 150.
Gillett, Alexander, 158.
Griswold, Stanley, 158.
Griswold, George, 36.
Graham, John, 33.
Gridley, Uriel, 174.
Gridley, Elijah, 144.

Hale, David, 144.
Hall, Samuel, 15.
Hall, Theophilus, 11.
Hart, Levi, 61.
Hart, Wm., 5.
Hawley, Stephen, 70.
Hawley, Rufus, 135.
Hemingway, Jacob, 5.
Hinsdale, Theodore, 78.
Higgins, David, 150.
Hosmer, Stephen, 11.
Hobart, Noah, 11.
Holmes, Stephen, 54.
Hooker, Nathaniel, 54.
Hotchkiss, Frederick W., 124.
Hunn, Nathaniel, 22.
Huntington, David, 158.
Huntington, Eliphalet, 69.

Huntington, Joseph, 54.
Huntington, Enoch, 54.

Ingersol, Jonathan, 31.

Judson, David, 36.
Johnson, Stephen, 78.
Johnson, Joshua, 124.

Kent, Elisha, 7.
Kellogg, Ebenezer, 104.
King, Walter, 150.
Kinne, Aaron, 101.

Langdon, Timothy, 139.
Lee, Andrew, 163.
Leonard, Joshua, 181.
Lewis, Isaac, 67.
Lee, Jonathan, 65.
Levinworth, Mark, 36.
Little, Ephraim, 7.
Lockwood, James, 45.
Lockwood, Samuel, 48.
Lockwood, William, 132.
Lothrop, Elijah, 65.
Lyman, William, 129.

Mansfield, Achilles, 124.
Marsh, Cyrus, 31.
Marsh, Jonathan, 117.
Marsh, John, 158.
Mason, Elijah, 65.
Mather, Moses, 28.
May, Eleazer, 104.
Merwin, Noah, 122.
Merrick, Jonathan, 39.
Mills, Gideon, 21.
Mills, Samuel J., 74.
Mills, Samuel, 168.
Miner, Jehu, 84.
Miner, Thomas, 112.
Miller, Jonathan, 158.
Mitchell, Justus, 117.
Murdock, Jonathan, 88.

Newell, Samuel, 30.
Newell, Abel, 48.
Nott, Abraham, 17.
Nott, Samuel, 117.

INDEX OF NAMES.

Norton, John, 31.
Noyes, John, 132.
Noyes, James, 144.

Parsons, Jonathan, 7.
Parsons, Elijah, 115.
Patten, William, 67.
Perkins, Nathan, 115.
Perry, Joseph, 50.
Pitkin, Timothy, 31.
Pomroy, Seth, 45.
Pomroy, Benjamin, 26.
Pond, Enoch, 158.
Prudden, Nehemiah, 158.

Rawson, Grindal, 36.
Rexford, Elisha, 107.
Ripley, David, 62.
Ripley, Hezekiah, 65.
Ross, Robert, 45.
Rosseter, Asher, 36.
Roots, Benajah, 69.
Robbins, Ammi R., 74.
Robinson, William, 144.
Roland, Henry A., 168.
Russell, William, 13.
Ruggles, Thomas, 5.

Salter, Richard, 48.
Seward, William, 52.
Sill, Elijah, 39.
Silliman, Robert, 69.
Sherard, Samuel, 45.
Skinner, Ichabod L., 174.
Smith, John Cotton, 67.
Smalley, John, 68.
Smith, Daniel, 168.
Starr, Peter, 99.
Stebbins, Stephen W., 119.
Stebbins, Samuel, 139.
Steele, Stephen, 9.
Strong, Joseph, 69.
Strong, Cyprian, 74.
Strong, Benjamin, 31.
Street, Nicholas, 101.
Strong, Nathan, 43.
Stone, Timothy, 109.

Storrs, William, 150.
Stores, Andrew, 74.
Stiles, Isaac, 7.

Taylor, Nathaniel, 45.
Tennant, Wm. M., 104.
Throop, Benjamin, 39.
Todd, Jonathan, 9.
Todd, Abraham, 43.
Trumble, Benjamin, 65.
Trumble, John, 25.
Tyler, Lemuel, 163.

Upson, Benoni, 129.

Vaill, Joseph, 132.

Waldo, Daniel, 174.
Wales, Samuel, 99, 124.
Warner, Noadiah, 62.
Wadsworth, Daniel, 11.
Waterman, Simon, 67.
Waterman, Elijah, 174.
Welch, Daniel, 74.
Welch, Moses Cook, 124.
Welles, Noah, 26.
West, Joel, 181.
Wetmore, Noah, 61.
Wetmore, Israhiah, 30.
Whitney, Josiah, 107.
Whitman, Elnathan, 5.
Whitaker, Nathanael, 48.
White, Stephen, 26.
Whittlesey, Samuel, Jr., 22.
White, Thomas, 9.
Whitefield, George, 17, 18.
Williams, Eleazer, 9.
Williams, Solomon, 9.
Williams, Warham, 62.
Williams, Eliphalet, 65.
Williams, Nathan, 99.
Willes, Henry, 19.
Willard, John, 67.
Williston, Noah, 112.
Worthington, William, 13.
Woodbridge, Samuel, 7.
Woodbridge, Ashbel, 7.
Woodbridge, Benjamin, 19.

www.ingramcontent.com/pod-product-compliance
Lightning Source LLC
Chambersburg PA
CBHW021734220426
43662CB00008B/849